HISTORIC FIFE

The West Shore at Pittenweem in the East Neuk of Fife.

HISTORIC FIFE

DUNCAN FRASER

M.A., F.S.A. SCOT.

MELVEN PRESS, PERTH

1982

Books by Duncan Fraser

LAND OF THE OGILVYS
MONTROSE BEFORE 1700
DISCOVERING ANGUS AND MEARNS
DISCOVERING EAST SCOTLAND
HIGHLAND PERTHSHIRE
PORTRAIT OF A PARISH
THE SMUGGLERS
FOUR HUNDRED YEARS AROUND KENMORE
GLEN OF THE ROWAN TREES
EAST COAST OIL TOWN
EDINBURGH IN OLDEN TIMES
THE FLOWER PEOPLE
HISTORIC FIFE

PRINTED IN GREAT BRITAIN BY
BUTLER & TANNER LTD, FROME AND LONDON

ISBN 0 906664 20 9

Acknowledgment

I SHOULD LIKE to warmly thank all those who have helped to complete this book by my late husband, Duncan Fraser. Duncan planned this book and wrote it and made many of the photographs for it, just as he did for his twelve previous books about Scotland, but he died before he could complete *Historic Fife*.

I owe its completion principally to George Knight of San Francisco, a writer and photographer who was a good friend of Duncan and is now my husband. He finished the last two chapters from research notes left by Duncan, took many of the photographs and designed the book to reflect the spirit of Duncan's other books.

Thanks are also due to Mr James Boyd and the staff of Dundee Museum for source material about Carpow and Tentsmuir, and to Kirkcaldy Museum for information on the Wemyss caves.

Of great value to this book are its photographs. Credit for those and copyright to them is as follows:—

Morris Allan, Dunfermline: page 17.
Scottish Development Department: pages 18, 32, 127.
National Trust for Scotland: pages 22, 24, 63, 64, 65, 173, 185.
A. D. S. Macpherson, Stirling: page 26.
Kirkcaldy Museum: pages 36, 37.
National Museum of Antiquities, Scotland: pages 39, 84.
Scottish Tourist Board: page 40.
C. M. Cowie, St Andrews: page 128.
Ken Hay, Montrose: page 147.
The Royal Commission on the Ancient & Historical Monuments of Scotland: pages 170, 171.
Barry Knight of Melven Press, Perth: page 178.
Dundee Museum: pages 182, 183, 186.

All other photographs were made by either George Knight or Duncan Fraser.

DORA KNIGHT.

DUNCAN FRASER   1905-1977

Contents

Now Fife is quickly reached by the road bridge across the Forth at Queensferry.

1

The Kingdom of Fife

WHEN THE road bridges were built, a few years ago, over the Forth and the Tay, people suddenly began to discover the long-forgotten wonderland that is the Kingdom of Fife. For many a century no other place in Scotland was quite as exciting to live in and it still has a heritage which is quite unique, though four hundred years have passed since the height of its fame.

You have to go back a long way to find the beginnings of life and death in Fife. It had its first known disaster some four hundred million years ago, at a time when the mountains of the Highlands were as high as the Himalayas. And that was long before man or monkey inhabited the earth. But even man came early to settle in Fife. About eight thousand years ago, when the entire population of Scotland numbered only a few hundreds, a coastal strip in North Fife was one of the rare abodes of those Stone Age settlers, the Mesolithic folk. It is still a good place for people who like shellfish, as they did.

Later, in Neolithic times and through the long centuries of the Bronze Age, the population was steadily growing. And then, almost two thousand four hundred years ago, a great wave of invaders from the Continent—the Gaelic-speaking Celts —swept triumphantly into Scotland to start a new Iron Age of progress. Their first foothold was on the shores of the

Tay. And up the estuary, where the hills of North Fife and Perthshire meet, the invaders covered the summits with mighty forts that are still clearly visible.

Centuries later the early Christian missionaries arrived and one of these was a monk called St Rule, from Patras in Western Greece. He brought a human armbone, three fingers from a right hand, one tooth and a knee-cap, all genuine parts of the skeleton of St Andrew. People liked a bit of a saint in those days.

Something else happened too that was even more memorable. When the local King of the Picts went down to the shore to find why the stranger had come to his realm, suddenly a great white cross appeared, shimmering diagonally in the clear blue sky. It was not the first time a king had seen such a vision. When Constantine the Great was about to march into battle in 306 A.D., he saw a similar cross inscribed in Greek: "By this sign you will conquer." The one over St Andrews Bay was wordless but still the cross became the national flag and the martyr of Patras the patron saint of Scotland. People did not know very much about this St Andrew. He was a far-off mystery man. But his bones were potent and that was what mattered.

Far better known, among the saints of Fife, was St Margaret, the Queen of Malcolm Canmore. Most of her life was spent in Southern Fife, at Dunfermline, then the capital of Scotland. There a shrine was erected in her memory soon after her death, and later she was given a more magnificent memorial, the great Benedictine Abbey which her son, David I, erected. The ashes of all but her head are still there.

Through most of the Middle Ages the Earls of Fife were first among the nobility of Scotland. They had the hereditary right to place the crown on the King's head at his coronation and to lead the vanguard of his army into battle. Fife too was the home of Scotland's leading churchman, the Archbishop of St Andrews, whose castle was close to the cathedral. The cathedral was by far the largest in the land, well over a hundred yards long.

It was here that higher education flourished for the first time in Scotland. Across the Border, foreign England had two Universities, Oxford and Cambridge. But Scots preferred to study overseas, until the one at St Andrews was founded in 1411. Among royal palaces, too, the first favourite of the Scottish monarchs for almost two centuries was Falkland Palace in Fife, built with a Renaissance grandeur that has been described as without parallel in the British Isles.

Fife in those days was noted not just for its palaces, its churchmen and its scholars. It was equally famed for its rich merchants and its thriving trade with the

The rail bridge stands in contrast to the modern motor span.

Continent. All along the East Neuk coast, crowded hard against each other, were the Royal Burghs and the burghs of barony that specialised in this overseas trade. They flourished at a time when ports farther south across the Forth were far too close to England for safety. And, in addition to the merchants and seamen on their peaceful missions, Fife produced a special breed of sea-dogs whose forays against the pirates of England kept the sea-lanes safe for the Scottish shipmasters.

Those East Neuk ports were prosperous, with sturdy little houses beside the sea-wall or up the narrow wynds that led so often from the shore to the High Street far above. It was the fisherfolk who lived in the wynds. The sea captains and the merchants had more spacious mansions, while the lairds loved the safety of castles. One of the special charms of Fife is the abundance of old houses, small and large, which still look as fresh today as when they were built long centuries ago.

But it was not all work and no play in those far-off days. In Fife is the oldest tennis court in Scotland, a royal one built for James V at Falkland Palace in 1539. There people still play real-tennis, which is tough and fast and very different from the tennis of today. In England the only court as old is at Hampton Court Palace. As for golf, there Fife has no equal in all the world. By 1552 the game had already become an obsession at St Andrews and it has remained one ever since.

Along the way to Dunfermline is the resting stone of St Margaret the Saxon.

2

Over
The Forth
And
Up Through
The
Kingdom

NOW, WITH the introductions finished, let us start on our journey from Edinburgh to South Queensferry and over the Forth Bridge into the Kingdom of Fife beyond.

Queen Margaret is said to have founded the ferry service which lasted for eight hundred years, between the Lothians and Fife, and certainly to her its terminals owe their ancient names of South and North Queensferry. The ferry was almost as ancient as Scotland itself. Older folk in her day could still remember when to cross from Fife to the Lothians was to voyage into a foreign land. If the first ferry crossing was a royal occasion, so too was the last, with Queen Elizabeth II on board, that day in 1964 when the Forth Road Bridge was opened.

St Margaret was a Saxon princess, a refugee from the Normans who had invaded her homeland. She was trying to reach the Continent when her ship was driven far off course, in a storm which brought her to the Firth of Forth. From Inverkeithing she set off on foot to seek the protection of Malcolm Canmore, in his royal palace at Dunfermline, and two and a half miles from her journey's end people still point to the "Saxon stone" on which she rested. It is a cup-marked stone slab, measuring 6 ft. 6 inches by 5 ft. 6 inches, and at that time — 1069 A.D.—was probably placed face uppermost on supports. Originally it had

been a sacred altar stone dating from pagan times. In 1856 it was raised to its present upright position and nearby is a farm that has long been known as St Margaret's Stone Farm.

Malcolm Canmore not only gave her protection. He fell in love with her and, although she had intended to enter a nunnery, she agreed to become his Queen.

All through her life there was never any doubt about her saintliness and many a miracle was credited to her.

North of Tower Hill and the ravine on which Dunfermline stands is St. Margaret's Cave. Tradition has it that Queen Margaret often retired here for secret devotion. Her husband, suspicious of her frequent visits to the cave, followed her and discovered her kneeling in prayer. Overjoyed that his suspicions were groundless, he had the Cave fitted up for her as a place of devotion. It consists of an apartment with one or two small recesses or niches in the sides of the rock and is a favourite place for pilgrims. In recent years, during the conversion of the Glen Bridge ravine, when a large car park was constructed, the cave was carefully preserved and a new entrance made which descends fifty-six feet from the car park. A large square stone in the form of a font, unearthed near the cave during the work, was placed inside.

[16]

Six Scottish Kings lie buried within historic Dunfermline Abbey.

Norman arches and Gothic windows show the antiquity of Dunfermline Abbey.

St Margaret's final resting place beside the Abbey.

The strangest of all the miracles connected with St Margaret came to light less than a century ago. Her biographer and confessor, Bishop Turgot, tells us that one of her specially treasured possessions was a little book, an illuminated manuscript of the Four Gospels, and he describes a remarkable misadventure it had. One day it was lost and, in spite of a thorough search, several hours passed before it was seen lying on the bed of a deep river. One of her courtiers dived in to retrieve it and incredibly it was almost completely undamaged. After her death it soon disappeared again and the Bishop's story passed into history as merely one of the myths that had grown up around her. But in 1887 an old manuscript found its way into the Bodleian Library and this was proved without any doubt to be her actual book. The lettering and the colourful illuminations had lost scarcely any of their brightness, though the faint traces of its immersion in the river could still be seen. And, to remove the last shadow of doubt, someone had described in verse how the book was lost and found again, and pasted it into the book. Though it was not written by Bishop Turgot, the story was very much the same and the handwriting contemporary.

Often Queen Margaret used to accompany her husband on his hunting trips to Edinburgh. They lived in a hunting lodge on the castle rock, for no castle was there in those days, and in it she died in 1093 A.D. With enemy troops closing in, her body was smuggled down the steep rock and across the river to Fife for burial in her beloved Dunfermline. And there she was laid to rest in a little church that had been built for her, beside the castle in Pittencrieff Glen.

Today on the site of her chapel stands the great abbey church which David I erected to her memory half-a-century after her death. Much of the present abbey was built long after his death, but his impressive nave with its massive pillars is still there to be admired. Probably it was from Durham that he brought the craftsmen who designed them and carved the vigorous Norman decorations above the west doorway. Such work is rare in Scotland, though two other fine examples can be seen at Leuchars in Fife and across the Forth at Dalmeny.

King David's nave and the great west door, however, are not the oldest parts of Dunfermline Abbey. The foundations of his mother's little church were rediscovered in modern times and these can now be seen through a grating.

There was an impressive ceremony at the abbey in 1259 A.D., when the body of St Margaret was taken from its original stone coffin and reburied close to the high altar in a shrine of pine wood set with gold and precious stones. It was a place

The North Porch of the Abbey was a very busy place of old.

of pilgrimage all through the Middle Ages. But with the coming of the Reformation holy relics were no longer safe. In 1567, it is said, her head was smuggled out of the grave and taken to Mary Queen of Scots. Then, for more than thirty years, it was hidden in the house of the Laird of Dury. Eventually it was taken to France, where it finally disappeared during the French Revolution.

St Margaret's Shrine is close to the east gable of the modern church, and nearby is all that remains of the Choir of the medieval Abbey.

From the Shrine, a path to the right leads to the North Porch, which was the entrance for the laity to the monastic church. Here baptisms and marriages were carried out, and the large cavities on both sides of the porch were

originally for alms boxes.

St Margaret was not the only royal person to be buried in Dunfermline Abbey. Six Scottish kings lie there as well, with the grave of Robert the Bruce beneath the pulpit. He was buried in the Abbey in 1329 but, over the years, the exact position of his grave became uncertain. Then in 1818, when the foundation of the New Abbey Church was being prepared, his tomb was rediscovered, the skeleton in a shroud of cloth of gold, and the breast-bone severed where his heart had been removed and taken to the Holy Land, in accordance with his wishes. He was reburied with ceremony and in 1889— 560 years after his death, his descendant, the Earl of Elgin, gifted memorial brass to mark the tomb.

King Robert the Bruce is well guarded by the Abbey pulpit.

The Study, Culross, built as a residence by Robert Leighton, Bishop of Dunblane.

Where only the gentry trod in old Culross.

All through its history the abbey had a royal palace beside it and, though the palace has now fallen into ruins, for centuries it was a favourite residence of the Kings of Scotland. David II and James I of Scotland and Charles I were all sons of Dunfermline.

At a street corner in the town is the house where another of its famous sons was born, the steel multi-millionaire Andrew Carnegie. His working class parents emigrated to America with him, when he was still a child, but he never forgot his native town. Much more of its rich cultural life today is due to him than to its three kingly sons.

*   *   *

Five miles to the south-west, the little old town of Culross climbs up from the shore of the Firth of Forth. Unique not only in Fife but in all Scotland, this is the Rip Van Winkle burgh where life has stood still for three centuries and more.

In sleepy surprise it surveys the oddly dressed folk who come trooping along the crown o' the causeway like gentry — and no one bothers to push them off the flat stones, back on to the cobbles where they belong. They go into the Study beside the Mercat Cross, and up the stairs to stare in wonderment at the ceiling with its painted decorations. You would think they had never seen such a ceiling before! They stare no less oddly at the fashionable windows, with their fixed leaded glass above and their shutters below. And they look so curiously at the Culross girdle in the fireplace. When Rip Van Winkle went to sleep there was scarcely a house in Scotland that did not possess one of these.

In the Study, built about 1600, is displayed a fascinating collection of old furniture, pottery, pewter and maps

[23]

Decorated ceilings were the vogue in fine homes.   The Study, Culross.

depicting centuries of domestic life in Culross. The tower contains a turnpike stair.

Outwardly Culross is still very much as it was in those olden days and many of its houses, restored in recent years, look as new as when they were first erected. One at least was there as early as 1577 and several others within the next half-century. Only the old brisk liveliness is missing. Culross was full of life in the days when the rich Bruces lived in their palace overlooking the busy Sandhaven that skirted the waterfront.

The Palace was built between 1597 and 1611 and has not been altered since its completion. The oldest part is the central building to the west of the court-yard, with the letters GB 1597 above the dormer window (for George Bruce). But the later part of the building has another dormer window with initials SGB 1611 (Sir George Bruce) after he received his knighthood. This remarkable man was descended from a noble family of Bruce prominent at the time of Bannockburn, and his house grew along with his mounting fortune. Even more interesting

The Mercat Cross is at the centre of the web of "Causeys" in Culross.

The old Town House of Culross rises over a sea of pantiled roofs.

than the buildings are the tempera and oil painted wood ceilings, walls and beams, now carefully and painstakingly restored. This design has become known as Scottish Renaissance Decorative Painting. The vaulted ceiling is divided into panels on which are painted quaint designs with Latin mottoes and a Scottish couplet below each one.

The original type of windows were also restored, with fixed leaded glass in the upper half and wooden shutters below.

In the long gallery or banqueting hall

[26]

OMNIS CARO FOENVM

SIRENES

Mens pleasures fond, do promeis only joyes,
Bot he that yeldes, at lenghe him self destroyes.

PATIENTIA OMNIÆ VINCIT

With patience suffer still,
and twin ye fall in fine:
C se fols subdue,
When they with shame fall
pyne.

Decoration and morality are impressively joined overhead at the Palace, Culross.

The glass came from Holland.   *The famous Culross girdle.*

you can see one of the original Culross girdles, distinguished by the handle, projecting straight from the edge, not curved from side to side as most Scottish girdles, and with the Royal Warrant mark of the Hammermen of Culross. Hanging in the fireplace is a swey, to hold the cooking pot in days gone by.

Being a royal burgh, it was a place where craftsmanship flourished. In the Abbey Churchyard, up on the hill, you can still see their trade insignia proudly displayed on their tombstones in readiness for the Judgment Day — the bakers, the weavers, the fleshers and hammermen of Culross. A baker had a biscuit and other bakery products, alongside a skull and crossbones. The crown and hammer were the insignia of the girdlesmiths, while a chopper and cleaver were used to depict the fleshing trade.

And down the side alleys in the burgh itself the constant clang of hammers echoed and re-echoed, for the girdlesmiths were always busy. They had a virtual monopoly of girdle-making in Scotland. But even their many workshops were overshadowed by Culross's major industries, the salt-pans and the coal mine

that Sir George Bruce owned. Luckily the prevailing wind blew over Culross before reaching the salt-pans. Otherwise the town would have been perpetually enshrouded in smoke. To obtain the salt, seawater was put into iron pans and a fire lit beneath them. The water had to be boiled eight times to produce salt suitable for curing. In 1663 Culross had fifty of these pans.

But the coal mine was even more famous than the extensive salt-pans. It was one of the wonders of Scotland. When James I paid a brief visit to his native land in 1617, Sir George's coal mine was one thing he specially wanted to see. And it was even more exciting than he had imagined. For a mile his host led him through an underground vault with nooks and crannies on either side, all man-made. He saw the miners producing tons of coal and one of the most impressive sights of all was the elaborate drainage system to get rid of the water which seeped in. Three horses drove an endless chain on which eighteen empty buckets were constantly moving down to gather the water, while other eighteen full buckets removed it outside.

But not even the King could remain

The swey is still ready today.

Tradesmen took trade seriously.

wholly unmoved, when the biggest surprise of all came at the far end of the vaulted tunnel. Emerging from the semi-darkness into the full light of day, he found himself away out on the Firth, with water all around and the shore a mile away. It was a most wicked conspiracy. "Treason, treason!" he screamed in a panic.

It all ended happily. The good Sir George had a boat waiting to take his Sovereign back to the shore and by evening the King was feeling well enough to relax at a banquet in Sir George's palace down by the waterfront, in an elegant room with painted walls and ceilings. It may have been on the same visit that the King climbed East Lomond Hill and when he saw the smoking salt-pans along the coast, exclaimed that Fife was "as a beggar's mantle fringed with gold".

Sir George's mine went on prospering for eight more years, sending weekly shipments of coal to Hamburg, and then a tremendous storm destroyed it.

On the crest of the hill overlooking the burgh is Culross Abbey, founded in 1217. The parts remaining are the eastern portion of the Abbey Church, which has served as the parish Church since 1633, the incomplete southern wall of its nave, and portions of the cloister buildings. The old cloister garth, behind the present manse, is now a garden.

Nearby is the Abbey House and its own beautiful garden, with a long terrace bordered by old-fashioned shrub roses, and almost unchanged from the time of the 17th century.

Inside the Abbey Church, in the Bruce Vault off the north transept is a remarkable alabaster monument of 1642 with finely detailed effigies of Sir George Bruce and his wife, lying in a niche, with their three sons and five daughters kneeling in front of the tomb.

The inscription reads:

"This is Sir George Bruce of Carnock, his lady, his three sons and five daughters. This tomb was provided by George Bruce of Carnock, his eldest son."

Si mortui non resurgunt
Neque Cristus resurexit
Resurexit autem et factus
Est primitial obdormentium aunn

"If the dead rise not, neither is Christ risen, but it is certain He has risen and become the first fruit of the sleepers."

The master merchant of Culross and his lady are eternally attended.

At the east end of Culross, by the roadside and close to the seashore, is St Mungo's chapel, now in ruins. This was the place where St Mungo (or Kentigern) was born when his mother landed by boat after being set adrift by her irate father. Educated by St Serf, St Mungo later became patron saint of Glasgow and founded its Cathedral. The little chapel was built in 1503 by Robert Blackadder, first Archbishop of Glasgow, in honour of St Mungo. The tree in Glasgow's seal is the hazel bush used by St Mungo when, as a boy, he lit the lamps at the monastery, and the bird in the Glasgow seal is the pet robin of St Serf, miraculously restored to life by St Mungo.

During the 17th century Culross still echoed to the hammer blows of the girdlesmiths. But by then, like many another burgh in Scotland, it was being sorely troubled by witches. They were becoming almost a public scandal. There was Mrs Craich, for example. When she was accused, she solemnly raised her hand in the air and swore to the magistrates that she was in fact no witch. She couldn't pull it down again. And there was another witch who was led to her execution from that same Town House prison. Though she had two legs, like most people, somehow she managed to leave just one single footprint on the turret stair. And that footprint survived into modern times.

There was yet another of them, a notorious one, who was locked up in the same turret prison in the 1640s. The weather was cold and raw, and the room unheated. So the warders locked her feet in the stocks and went off to another room, where they could sit in comfort by the fire. Suddenly they heard a wild shriek and a sickening thud, and when they rushed outside they found her spreadeagled on the roadway and near to death. Both her legs were broken, so four men had to carry her on a chair to her execution a few days later. But, at least, the crowds were not disappointed. People came even from across the Forth to see her burning.

There was a public enquiry, of course, and it was proved that she had not actually jumped from her prison. While the warders were away, the Devil had slipped in and released her. He pulled her through the window and was carrying her off to safety, when she suddenly took fright and fell. She would never have been any good on a broomstick.

But if you think Culross was bad for witches, you should take a look at Torryburn, only a mile and a half away. It was worse.

The roots of Glasgow reach across to the ruins of this shrine at Culross.

Inchcolm Abbey, on an island near Aberdour, is called "The Iona of the West".

3

Wemyss Caves and Pictish Relics

THERE ARE other ancient towns along the coast. Inverkeithing has a 12th century church, a 14th century monastery and several houses of the 16th century. Aberdour's old castle is partly 14th century, and its parish church had its beginnings as early as the one at Inverkeithing.

Inchcolm Abbey, just south of Aberdour, is situated on the small island of St Colme's Inch, named after St Columba, who lived here for a time, according to tradition. The monastery buildings include a 13th century octagonal chapter house.

At Kinghorn, a monument marks the spot where, in the 13th century, King Alexander III fell to his death while riding home from Edinburgh along a clifftop path.

Burntisland claims to be the oldest of these towns, with its origins in Roman times. But older still are the famous caves at East Wemyss, between Kirkcaldy and Leven. There you will find Britain's earliest picture of a boat, as well as hunting scenes, portrayed by craftsmen of Pictish times.

Those remarkable caves were carved by the sea in the sandstone cliffs long after Scotland emerged from its Ice Age.

In 1746 a Jacobite fugitive, the Chevalier Johnstone, spent a night in one of them while trying to escape abroad after the Battle of Culloden. But he found it an unnerving experience.

Not every visitor to the Wemyss caves has shared the Chevalier's terror. In the daytime the caves have an enchantment that they lack at night. Even royalty has fallen under their spell. James IV was so impressed by one of them that he held court there and it is known as the Court Cave. But the Picts were there long before the King and on its walls can be seen the symbols they carved more than a thousand years ago — crude versions of the ones which recur so often on cross slabs, farther north in Angus and East Perthshire. There are cup-markings, too, probably Bronze Age. And one very special carving in the Court Cave is of the Viking god Thor with his great hammer and his sacred goat; a reminder that there were artists as well as plunderers among the Norsemen.

In another of the caves, Jonathan's Cave, is a carving of a boat, probably a Pictish one, and pictures of animals and birds.

Nine of those caves are known by name, but unfortunately, in nearly all of them, danger has kept looming up over the years and a quite remarkable variety of troubles befell them, for they are in very friable stone formations. One of them, a century ago, was the White Cave, large and impressive until its entrance was built up for safety. There was the

Glass Cave, for centuries the largest of them all. Soon after the Michael Colliery was opened nearby, the cave was undermined and collapsed in 1904 with a mighty roar. At that time the Doo Cave was not one but two. The inner one, almost as large as the Glass Cave, was nearly a hundred feet long and almost as high, with a width of almost sixty feet. But now there is no inner cave. During the First World War a gun emplacement was built on top and when the gun was fired the roof of this inner cave collapsed. The outer cave too was damaged in 1937 by a stormy sea. And there was the Michael Cave, silted up and almost forgotten, which returned to the limelight for a few brief hours in 1929 because a boiler seat at the Michael Colliery was giving trouble. A crack below revealed a hole in the cave roof through which the ancient carvings could be seen. Photographs were hurriedly taken before the crack was filled with concrete.

It was not only in the caves, however, that Fife's Pictish relics were preserved. For many a long century much richer treasures were to be found eight miles farther north around Largo Law. There used to be a rich mine of gold on this hill. You could have guessed that from the sheep that grazed there, for every time one of them lay above the treasure its fleece got a golden tinge. But if you

Jonathan is one of the better preserved of the Wemyss Caves.

Seen as a dog and possibly a trident.

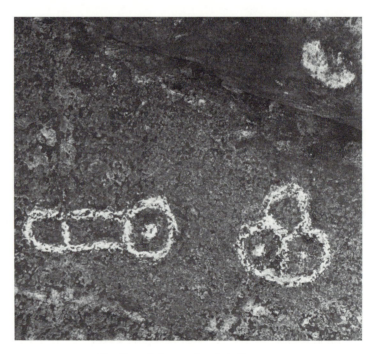

On the right, a dumb-bell.

Seen as a Pictish sceptre of authority.

Thor with his hammer and sacred goat.

wanted to dig up this gold and be rich beyond your dreams, it was impossible to find the exact spot just by watching the sheep. You had to enlist the help of a local ghost, who had promised that

If Auchindownie cock disna craw
And Balmain horn disna blaw,
I'll tell you where the gowd mine is
    in Largo Law.

Centuries passed before a shepherd with a passion for wealth decided to risk the possible hazards. He began by killing every cock, old and young, at Auchindownie. Then he contacted his friend Tammie Norrie, who was the cow-herd at Balmain, and made him promise not to blow his horn while bringing in the cattle. The ghost kept his part of the bargain. He materialised before the very eyes of the excited shepherd and together they set off for the spot where the treasure lay hidden. But things still went wrong. The quiet of the twilight hour was shattered by the note of the cow-herd's horn, for Tammie alas had forgotten.

The shepherd never recovered from the shock. Before the ghost vanished it struck him dead, leaving him rooted so firmly to the spot that no one could move his body. His friends covered him up with a cairn of stones that eventually turned into a green hillock as the grass spread over it. It is still an uncanny spot.

As for the treasure, it was not actually on Largo Law at all, but on nearby Norrie's Law. A tinker discovered that, when he was digging for sand about 1819. There are differing stories about what he actually found. Some say it was a stone coffin containing a suit of scale armour, with a shield, scabbard and sword handle all of silver. Others maintain it was a hoard consisting mainly of finely made goblets and other vessels of silver. The tinker anyway did a profitable business with a silversmith in Cupar, who melted them down for their metal. Almost everything vanished before word of the find got around. But eventually the site was examined by experts. So, in the National Museum of Antiquities in Edinburgh, you can still see a few relics which escaped the tinker's eye.

By far their most interesting feature is their ornamentation. Here too, as in the caves at Wemyss, the decoration is Pictish, but much more finely done. It includes the same kind of symbols—the 'spectacles' and 'Z-rod', the mirror and maybe even the sea-horse—that you find on the Pictish stones at Aberlemno and elsewhere. Such symbols on metalwork ornaments are very uncommon. But they also help to date the hoard. It had lain buried there for about a thousand years before the tinker found it.

A Pictish treasure which escaped the tinker's eye.

Elie's harbour is leisurely now, compared with the early busy times of trade.

4

The
Picture-book
East Neuk

ONE OF the most colourful corners of all Scotland is the East Neuk of Fife that looks out over the broad Firth of Forth to the Lothians beyond. It is a picture-book land with its little houses and the smell of the sea and, in a world where to conform has become important, this is still the land of the individualists.

Not for them the houses of other places, streamlined and modern, outside and in, like peas in a pod. They like theirs to be snug and pretty and different from their neighbours'. And being different is an old East Neuk custom. You might think at first glance that all those houses had survived from the 16th or 17th century. Many of them have, in fact, with their red pantiled roofs, their crow-stepped gables and colour-washed walls. It was the local stone that made the folk turn to colour. Because the stone was inclined to be soft in Fife, they had to lime-wash their houses. And colour looks well on a lime-washed wall, especially if it is different from the one next door. So you got those walls of cream and yellow, pale blue, pink and grey, and snowy white, with black or contrasting colours round the windows and doors.

But it was not only in their taste for colour that the folk of the East Neuk were individualists. They liked outside stairs of solid stone. They lent a touch of character to a house, and no planner

Robinson Crusoe in Lower Largo.

would have dared to come along and tell them to remove it. About windows too they were particular. They didn't like the modern labour-saving way, where all the windows are exactly the same in size and each in its proper place. Not living in the Affluent Society, they could afford a little luxury! And so they made their windows of different sizes and staggered them along the wall for better effect. Most of all they liked their new house to have a handsome doorpiece, richly moulded, with maybe a plaque above, showing the initials of the owner and his wife and the year when they built it. Sometimes, instead, they put an anchor on the plaque or a ship in full sail. You can study the changes in ships through the years just by looking at some of those plaques.

The sea was the life-blood of the East Neuk towns. And there were plenty of those towns—Royal Burghs and burghs of barony—drawing a livelihood from it. Crail, Anstruther Easter, Anstruther Wester, Pittenweem, St Monans, Elie, Earlsferry and Largo were all seaports with a Continental trade, in a fifteen-mile stretch of coastline.

*   *   *

Largo is more noted for its seafarers than for its buried treasure. It was the home of two very famous seamen—the illustrious Admiral Sir Andrew Wood,

terror of the English navy, and the more humble Alexander Selkirk who in his boyhood was something of a terror, too. Selkirk's adventures inspired Daniel Defoe to write "Robinson Crusoe", and also induced the authorities at Juan Fernandez to rename their western island Isla Alejandro Selkirk and their eastern one Isla Robinson Crusoe.

Incidentally, it is claimed that the umbrella was invented by a Largo man, and that is why it was known for so long as a "Nether Lairgie". Alexander Selkirk had an umbrella, so Daniel Defoe gave Crusoe one on his desert island.

It was in a little cottage down by the shore at Lower Largo that Selkirk spent his boyhood. By the age of fifteen he was already a strapping lad, the proud possessor of a dangerous pistol and an even more dangerous temper. So there was a chain reaction one day when by mistake he drank some salt water. He thrashed his brother Andrew for laughing and had thoughts of blowing his brains out. But their father, an honest shoe-maker and a church elder, put a stop to that. Sitting down on the floor, with his back to the door that led up to the garret, he prevented Alex reaching his pistol. A married brother heard the uproar and came rushing from his house along the road. A few minutes later the sister-in-law followed, just in time to release her

[43]

husband and old Mr Selkirk from the teenager's iron grasp. "You false loon," she yelled, "will ye murder your father and my husband both?" The minister and the rest of the kirk session were black affronted when they heard of it.

Alex went to sea after that, for he had excellent prospects in the privateering trade. In 1704 he set off for the South Seas as a sailing master in the vessel Cinque Ports, of about 40 tons, with 16 guns and a crew of 63. But that was an unlucky venture. They found no trace of the two Spanish galleons they had hoped to capture with booty worth £600,000. Then the captain died, leaving a successor who was far from popular. More than forty of the crew refused to sail under him and went ashore on Juan Fernandez. Though that trouble was patched up, Selkirk himself had a violent quarrel with him eight months later and went ashore alone on the same uninhabited land. It was September 1704.

Almost four years passed before some Bristol merchants fitted out a couple of privateering vessels to cruise in the South Sea. The Duke, commanded by Captain Woodes Rogers, R.N., carried 30 guns and the Dutchess (sic) 26 guns. Between them they had 333 sailors, mostly foreigners, and "near one half of her Majesty's subjects on board were tinkers, tailors, Welsh hay-makers, North British pedlars, Irish fiddlers and pipers, one negro and about ten boys". On their way south they seized a small Spanish barque.

Selkirk saw the two ships approaching the island and, lighting a fire to attract their attention, ran along the shore to meet them. One of the crew described him as "swift as a native goat" and the phrase was apt. His jacket, breeches and cap were all of goatskin. Even the sewing was with goatskin thongs. He slept in a goatskin bed. Almost inaccessible rocks had to be climbed to reach the tree-shaded spot where he had built his hut with its bedroom and kitchen, and when the sailors reached this wooden cabin they found tame goats grazing round the door.

So his four years and four months on the island came to an end. He took his seaman's chest, his musket and one of his long knives, and joined the privateers. Within six months he was master of a 50-ton prize and by September the following year he was master of the Duke, the biggest ship of the three. In 1711 he was back in Britain with £800 as his share of the booty.

The story goes that one Sunday, in the spring of 1712, he returned to Lower Largo dressed in such elegant gold-laced clothes that even his mother failed for a time to recognise him. Before he went south again he gave her his gun, his clothes chest and a drinking cup he had made on the island from a coconut shell.

The trace of the old sea-dog's canal at Upper Largo.

These, in later years, were the star exhibits when visitors came to the cottage. And they came in vast numbers. Among them was Sir Walter Scott, who borrowed the drinking cup to have a rosewood stand made for it in Edinburgh, with the inscription: "The cup of Alex Selkirk, whilst in Juan Fernandez, 1704-9."

In 1885 the humble cottage was replaced by a more substantial modern building and a statue of the traditional Robinson Crusoe, looking out to sea, was erected in a niche over the doorway. It can still be seen there.

*   *   *

Just a mile from the Kirkton of Largo, on the foothill of Largo Law, was the castle of Sir Andrew Wood, Commander of the Yellow Carvel and the Flower, and scourge of the English navy. With only those two ships, in 1481, he drove invading squadrons of English warships out of the Forth and Clyde. His achievements grew with the years. In 1489 he captured several English cruisers. Next year he added a further eight to his list.

In those days there was a certain jollity about fighting that is sorely lacking today. In 1490, three English warships hid behind the Isle of May, off the Fife coast, waiting to ambush him, and when his two ships were seen approaching, the English captain "gart peirse the wyne and drank a toast with all his skippers and captains".

Then the battle began. As the Yellow Carvel and the Flower found the trap closing round them, Sir Andrew rapped out his orders. The gunners charged their artillery and crossbows; the lime pots and fireballs were hoisted aloft; those with two-handed swords went up in front; and then came a rousing speech from Sir Andrew that all must fight for the honour of the realm. Then,

[45]

without more ado, he "caussit to fill the wyne and everie man drank to wther". And so they proceeded to demolish the English.

At Largo Sir Andrew has left more than just a memory of his famous victories. One tower of his castle has survived, overlooking what is in fact the dried-up bed of a canal. One end of this canal can still be clearly seen in a hollow in the park, behind the castle. The first of the wells which fed it is there too, and two or three others along the route. There were several more, at one time, but these were filled in because they were a danger to cattle.

The mile-long route of Sir Andrew's canal can still be easily traced from his castle along the hillside to Largo Church. It served an excellent purpose. When the old sea-dog was too old to ride to mass on horseback, he sailed there along his canal in a private barge manned by eight oarsmen.

*   *   *

At Elie, with its narrow wynds leading down to the sea, the great James Braid, five times winner of the open golf championship, spent his boyhood and learned his golf. And east of the harbour is a stone structure which looks at first glance like a ruined castle but isn't. This is the Lady's Tower, a relic of the days when ladies and class barriers were mighty. A noted Fife beauty, Lady Janet

Anstruther, used to go bathing here and the tower was built for her. Everyone in Elie knew when Lady Janet was having a bathe. She sent the bellman round the streets to warn the inhabitants to stay away.

In spite of her beauty the story goes that she brought a curse on the House of Elie. Between Elie House and Kinconquhar Loch was the village of Balclevie, where the people had an annoying habit of gathering each morning and evening, to hold a outdoor religious service. And scarcely less irritating was the way their houses blocked her view of the loch. So she persuaded her husband to demolish the village. And that brought a curse upon her.

Elie's twin town is the much more ancient Earlsferry, which got a new charter in 1589 and was described even then as "old beyond the memory of man". There are three caves in the rock face at Kincraig Point—the Deil's Cave, the Doo's Cave and the spectacular Macduff's Cave, where the Thane of Fife is said to have hidden from Macbeth's assassins, until fishermen rowed him across the Forth to safety. There is a tradition that Malcolm Canmore repaid Macduff's loyalty by decreeing that anyone suspected of crime must not be pursued from Earlsferry till he was halfway across the Forth.

[46]

Lady Janet's private bathing tower at Elie.

The sea-weathered Church of the fisher folk at St Monans.

5

World of the Fisher Folk

NORTHWARD, OFF the main road, is the ancient fishtown of St Monans. In the old days, no stranger ever passed that way unnoticed. Though the folk were never by nature over-curious, there was a sure guarantee that an unknown face would bring every villager to his door, to gaze. So the story got around: "If a stranger cam' in wice at the tae end o' the toun he'll gang oot daft at the ither."

You had to like insects if you lived in St Monans. Everyone knew that to kill a spider or a hornie golach was sure to bring bad luck. But one had to be careful about many things. No one would dream of asking where a herring boat was going to fish, though where she *had* fished was a question that could do no one any harm.

But St Monans was by no means unique in that. It was not even unique in having a long list of unmentionable words—like rats, hares and rabbits, pigs, pork, salmon and ministers — though certainly it had good reason for avoiding all those words. Take rabbits, for example! One day the crew of a St. Monans boat landed on the Isle of May and foolishly went rabbit-hunting. On the journey back they were caught in a storm and not one escaped alive. That showed what rabbits could do.

It was an ill-omen too if you met a woman, when you were in your fishing clothes and on your way to the sea. But to meet the minister at such a time was even more unlucky. And that may seem odd, for the ancient church at the end of the town has always been very much a part of St Monans.

No other church in Scotland is quite so close to the sea. In winter's storms the swirling spray hurls itself over the churchyard wall, on to the graves and up to the very door itself. Inside are further reminders of the sea. A handsome model of a full-rigged ship hangs above your head in the transept. A 130 gun Frigate of 1750-1800, it was presented to the church by Captain Marr, a native of St Monans. His ship had earned prize money, but by the time it was paid, his crew had been dispersed, so he used the money to provide a model of his ship, which he gifted to his church. At the time of the church restoration in 1828 the model was sold to an Edinburgh artist. Ultimately it was bought back from his widow and restored by St Monans boatbuilder Thomas Miller before being rehung in the old church.

At the far end of the choir is a large replica of the old seal of St Monans —four men in a boat with the warning "Grip fast" and the motto "Mare vivimus" (By the sea we live). The story behind the design is that Bartholomew, the founder of the family of Leslie, was Governor of Edinburgh Castle in 1067, and was also Lord Chamberlain to Queen Margaret. One of his duties was to carry the Queen pillion on his horse. For safety, he wore a leather belt for the Queen to grip. On one occasion while crossing a stream, he cried out to the Queen "Grip fast!" and she replied "Gin the buckle bide!"

The church bell was a problem for a time. It brought bad luck when it was rung in the steeple, so it was taken out and hung from a tree in the churchyard instead. There was no more trouble until the herring season came round. But then, it was found, the shoals were frightened away by the sound, so the beadle had to stand at the church door and ring a less noisy handbell instead.

In those days now past, it was not an easy task being the minister of St Monans. The very word "minister" was high in the list of unmentionables and he had to get accustomed to something more harmless, like "the fellow who lives at so-and-so" or "the fellow with the black coat" or, more concisely, "the queer fellow". Meeting him on the way to sea was as bad as meeting a pig. There was only one way of breaking the spell — to avoid all work until the tide had ebbed and flowed.

It was the same with pigs. An entire crew perished after seeing one of them and there were several hairsbreadth escapes. Yet the inhabitants of the Uppertown still persisted in keeping pigs.

[50]

To honour seamen.

When the Nethertown folk could bear it no longer, they seized their boat-hooks and went marching up the hill to annihilate the pigs and their owners, if need be. But the Uppertown people were cunning. Gathering their swine, they drove them at the approaching fishermen, who fled back downhill in a panic.

While they waited for another tide to ebb and flow, the laird—the famous Sir David Leslie — peacefully solved the problem. Placing a total ban on the keeping of pigs in the Uppertown, he then let the fishermen into a secret. Scientists had discovered a new way to stop bad luck. There was no longer any need to wait for the ebb and flow, or rush to the church door and call the name of the saint. If you said "Touch cauld iron" and suited your action to the words, that was just as effective. It made "pigs" and "swine" quite harmless. And he was right. There was no more trouble in their lifetime.

Almost a century later, however, it did recur when a visiting minister preached in the church and chose for his text the parable of the prodigal son. That was enough to revive all the old memories. As he reached "he sent him into the fields to feed swine" there was a sudden fumbling and bending all over the church as they searched for nailheads to touch, and a mumbling of "Touch cauld iron". And a few moments later the cry rose again, even louder and more urgent, as the word "swine" kept recurring in his sermon. When he reached "the husks that the swine did eat", the congregation had had enough. In obvious agitation they fled from the church. It was most bewildering for the unfortunate minister.

Apart from its handsome church, St Monans still has many other links with those busy days of superstition. For over two centuries the Miller family has been there, building fishing boats and in olden times there was no lack of local customers, for St Monans itself once had 135 open boats. Those days are long since past but boats from this yard find their way to many parts of the world.

Round the harbour, too, are the picturesque houses of long ago, now restored to add their beauty to one of

There is a royal story behind this seal.

the most delightful towns in the East Neuk.

Two miles beyond St Monans is another East Neuk fish town, in some ways the most delightful of them all. Since Pittenweem is a very small town with a very big fishing fleet, one must expect a certain daily bustle there, as the boats get ready for the sea. There is an excitement too when the fleet returns and the catch is being landed. All roads then lead to the fish market. Time never hangs heavy on your hands in Pittenweem.

The fishermen's houses too have such an air of well-being that you would almost think in this technological age the old skills can still be rewarding. To fish successfully is in fact one of the oldest of all the skills in Pittenweem. It was mastered over eight hundred years ago.

If fishing is a feature of this East Neuk burgh, so is the ample car park at the shore. It is typical of that shrewdness for which Fife is famous. And Fife, after all, is the only place in the world where the hens lay their eggs in silence! The car park shows the same innate cunning as the hens. It is at one end of the shore, close to the handsome houses of the shipmasters of old, and overlooking the busy harbour. So visitors who park there for the first time—and maybe even for the twenty-first! — become so interested in their immediate surroundings that they never reach the other end of the front to find what is round the corner. That is why the loveliest part of Pittenweem remains quiet and peaceful —the West Shore with its old sea wall twisting in and out in front of a picture-book row of houses.

But even if you never reach the West Shore you will surely get as far as the wynds, those narrow closes which are the main thoroughfare of the town. Wynds like these are a feature of nearly all the East Neuk burghs but in Pitten-weem they have a rather special character because here they are so much steeper than elsewhere. And they are more ancient than any of the houses by the sea-wall.

In one of those wynds is by far the oldest house in Pittenweem — the God-made home of St Fillan. If you ask who St Fillan was, you raise a rather difficult question. There was a St Fillan who gave his name to the town of St Fillans in Perthshire. Another of the same name was a potent healer, who left a magic pool in the River Dochart and a set of healing stones that can still be seen in Killin. The saint of Pittenweem was neither of these. But it was apparently in the 7th century that the holy man lived in this cave and all through the Middle Ages pilgrims came to see the place where he used to live in Cove Wynd. A priory at the top of the wynd provided hospitality for the pilgrims. And no doubt they were impressed by the great house of this priory, for it was then a very handsome building, as it still is. The home of St

Fillan, however, was only a humble cave. From the entrance, it slopes downwards. The inner cave is in two parts, with a little altar in the right-hand portion and in the left side is a spring and holy well. The outer cave contains the saint's bed and fireplace. This primitive dwelling gave Pittenweem its name, for in the Pictish tongue, the word means "the place of the cave."

Not even a saint or a priory, however, could persuade the townsfolk to special-ise entirely in religious matters. All through the years the sea was in their blood and for centuries they had a Continental shipping trade which was in fact far more valuable than their fishing.

A shipmaster of Pittenweem took the fugitive Charles II to France after his defeat at Worcester in 1651. The mansion which this Captain Cook built for himself, on the waterfront overlook-ing the harbour, looks as fresh today as when he built it. Called The Gyles, it was beautifully restored by the National Trust for Scotland.

But Charles II also knew Pittenweem. He was there only a few months before his escape to France and a grand feast the townspeople gave him! There were "great buns" washed down by various wines, including canary and sack, and ale for those who preferred it. Probably he remembered the tablecloth too, for it was very handsome, a turkey red carpet

The entrance at Cove Wynd.

that Lord Kellie sent down from his castle behind the town.

Through most of the following century, Pittenweem's overseas trade continued. And a great deal of it was with Scandinavia. The old granaries, where the grain was stored while awaiting shipment, have not yet entirely disappeared from the town. They remind us of the time when almost half the ships that sailed into the Baltic from Scotland were from Fife and specially from the twin East Neuk ports of Pittenweem and Anstruther. It was in the first decade of the eighteenth century that the trade reached its peak. Then, those two ports together were sending far more ships to the Baltic than Glasgow and almost three times as many as Leith.

Pittenweem in those days had a prosperous air, just as it has today. But it had more rowan trees than most towns. You would meet folk wearing a sprig of it, almost any day of the year, and on May Day especially nearly everyone wore it. You would notice that they tied it with a red thread, as their forefathers had done for longer than anyone could remember. Maybe too you would notice that on six days of the week they would cut their finger-nails or toe-nails without a moment's worry about the consequences—but never on a Tuesday. It was not that they were superstitious.

One just had to be careful, when there were so many witches around.

If Pittenweem had been a farming instead of a seafaring community, things would have been different. The milk might go sour or the barn catch fire or someone turn sickly, if a witch took a spite at a farmer. But in a seafaring town the hazards were truly enormous, for witches could raise storms and cause shipwrecks and drownings and destitution for widows and orphans.

The year 1643—the year when everyone was signing the Solemn League and Covenant—was a specially bad one. In Fife alone about forty witches had to be burned in a matter of months and several of them belonged to Pittenweem. There were Mrs Dawson and Mrs Crombie, and the wives of Archibald and Thomas Wanderson, and the mother-in-law of George Hedderwick. In their case the authorities charged each of the husbands £80 Scots to help meet the cost of their burning. It was hoped that this would discourage others. But still each new generation produced more witches. It reached such a scandalous state that in

The cave at Pittenweem where, according to local folk, St Fillan lived.

1705 the townspeople lost all patience. They seized Janet Cornfoot, put a heavy door on top of her and loaded it with boulders until she was crushed to death. The Government, not understanding the problem, thought she should have been put on trial instead and were most annoyed.

But if Pittenweem had been offered a statue to its most exciting personality, it was not a witch or a witch-hunter or even one of its lairds who would have been chosen for the place on the pedestal. For sheer inspiration there was none to compare with a humble Fife smuggler. He fired the imagination not only of local folk but of tens of thousands all over Scotland.

Andrew Wilson was a baker in the village of Pathhead before he turned to full-time smuggling. He was tall, broad and brawny, and few smugglers around Pittenweem and neighbouring Anstruther were better known than he was, in the early 1730's. The only trouble was that the Customs officials knew him almost as well as his fellow-smugglers did, and time after time he was caught with goods that were duly confiscated.

The last time that happened was in James Wilson's tavern in the High Street of Anstruther—the one that was known in the trade as the Smugglers' Howff, before it was demolished. That seizure left Andrew destitute but it also inspired him to work out a very sensible plan for recovering his losses. Altogether the Customs officers had robbed him of goods worth hundreds of pounds and the obvious way to get it back was to rob the Kirkcaldy Collector on one of his tours of the out-stations. So with three smuggling cronies, he arranged to settle the account next time the Collector was in Pittenweem.

Soon the opportunity came. The Collector on his visits used to lodge in Marygate, in one of the more picturesque houses in the town, and he had already retired for the night when the four arrived at his door. One of them, Geordie Robertson, stayed outside on guard with his cutlass in his hand, while the others burst in. In an uproar loud enough to waken the dead, the Collector jumped out of the bedroom window and

Pittenweem harbour, home port for an active fishing fleet.

fled in his nightshirt, while the smugglers pocketed the £200 he had left behind.

The street was by no means deserted. Several people heard the commotion and asked Geordie what was happening. He swung his cutlass with a nonchalant air and assured them that there was nothing to worry about. The Collector was merely having a quarrel with the other people who lived there. And that seemed reasonable enough, for it was a town where Customs officials were not ultra-popular.

But the Collector's escape spoiled everything. He roused the soldiers and a search began, and soon the luckless Wilson and his three companions were under arrest. One of them turned King's evidence at the trial, and Wilson and Robertson were condemned to death.

As they lay in the death cell in the Tolbooth of Edinburgh, a file and other tools were smuggled in and they managed to remove a bar from the window. Geordie, being the smaller of the two, suggested that he should slip through and widen the hole from the outside to let Wilson follow. But Wilson had a feeling that Geordie might forget about him and vanish as soon as he was out. He insisted on going first and got jammed so hard that he was still stuck fast when the guards arrived on their nightly round, a considerable time later. There were sleepless nights for Wilson after

that, as he lay tormented by the thought that through his folly his friend was now facing death.

On the last Sunday before the execution, the two condemned men were taken under armed guard to the Tolbooth Church, as the custom was, to join the congregation in worship. It was felt to be a benefit not only to the prisoners but to the whole congregation. And there was a specially solemn moment when the minister turned to the prisoners, in the special pew where they sat apart, each with an armed guard on either side, and bade them repent before they met their Maker.

When the service ended, many of the congregation lingered on to gaze in fascinated horror at the two condemned men. And then something quite unexpected happened. With onlookers all around, Wilson suddenly seized his own two guards in his iron grasp and, with a cry of "Run, Geordie, run!", hurled himself on top of one of Robertson's guards and dug his teeth into his collar. For a moment his friend remained rooted to the floor but members of the congregation now took up the cry and that brought him back to reality. Shaking off his remaining guard, he

"Rotten Row" saw much of smugglers and Andrew Wilson in his day.

How the fishing nets

were drawn up for repair.

leapt over the pew and was lost from sight among the crowd at the doorway. No one tried to stop him. When he was outside he vanished, never to be seen by the authorities again.

As for Wilson, he made no attempt to escape. His generous deed turned him into a public hero and a wave of sympathy swept through the country. There was no hope of a reprieve but it was rumoured that a rescue bid might be made, when he arrived at the Grassmarket for his execution. Hearing of this, the authorities sent eighty men of the City Guard, under their commander Captain John Porteous, to see that the scaffold claimed its victim. The execution took place as planned.

When Wilson was dead, however, the crowd became restless. There were shouts and angry scenes round the soldiers. Porteous ordered his men to fire and with his own first shot he killed a man. Six or seven others were dead and many wounded, before the Guard stopped shooting. Since several people of better rank were among the dead, Captain Porteous was tried, found guilty of wilful murder and condemned to be hanged.

It was the delay of his execution which led to the second of the Porteous Riots. On the night when he should have died, shadowy figures began to approach the Edinburgh Tolbooth from all directions. Some, it was said, were dressed like seafaring men with sailors' jackets and sea-caps. Others looked like women, though their stride was long and their voices deep and gruff. The gates leading to the Grassmarket were seized and locked. A band of armed men broke into the Tolbooth and dragged out the terrified Captain Porteous. He was half-carried down to the Grassmarket.

At dawn next morning the only signs of the night's events were an empty cell in the Tolbooth and a corpse dangling from a dyer's pole in the Grassmarket. The authorities were highly incensed. But though more than two hundred suspects were questioned in the next six weeks the only two who were brought to trial were found not guilty.

One thing, however, is certain. The last few days of Andrew Wilson's life assured him a fame he never had in all the years before. For a time it seemed that through his death Scotland might even break off the uneasy Union it had made with England in 1707. And no other smuggler in Scotland's history has ever done anything to compare with that. Pittenweem had some cause to feel proud of its humble part in that adventure.

Pittenweem rises steeply up from the waterfront.

[61]

A' Pittenweem Wynd.

Tracery in the Vine Room at Kellie Castle.

Three miles inland from Pittenweem is Kellie Castle, one of those rare old buildings that were designed not for feuding but for gracious living. Nothing very bloody ever happened there but it is still a joy to see the craftsmanship which gives it its special distinction.

Not many castles have so old a history. Once the barony of Kellie belonged to the Siwards, whose Saxon ancestors were noblemen in England before the Norman Conquest. Then came the Oliphants. It is just possible that the first of them, Sir Robert, built the oldest part of the present castle, the stone-vaulted ground floor of the north tower. There was royal blood in the veins of all Sir Robert's descendants, for he married a daughter of King Robert the Bruce.

Today the oldest part of the castle is only ten feet high. The rest of the north tower was rebuilt some time in the Middle Ages and later another tower was added to the south of it. You had to cross about fifty feet of open ground to get from the one tower to the other. And when the 4th Lord Oliphant succeeded to the title in 1573 the gap was still there. He added the "link building" which now joins the two together. It took thirty years to build and some of its finest features were not added until half-a-century after that. By then the Oliphants had sold the castle to Viscount Fenton, who became the first Earl of Kellie in 1619.

In the 1660s the plasterers moved into

[63]

A long history is elegantly preserved in Kellie Castle.

Kellie Castle. They left Lord Kellie the proud possessor of four of the most magnificent plasterwork ceilings in Scotland — in the Great Hall and the Withdrawing Room, and in the two bedrooms above. Even now, three centuries later, they are still outstanding examples of craftsmanship.

Finest of all is the Vine Room, where the sloping sides of the deeply coved ceiling are decorated with entwined vines, laden with fruit. A painting of Mount Olympus, in the centre, is by the seventeenth century Dutch artist De Wet, who was then making his mark in Scotland.

The plasterwork ceilings, however, are not the only notable features from this period. About the same time the Earl had the wall of the Withdrawing Room lined with decorative panelling in a style which was then the height of fashion.

There are sixty-four panels, all painted with romantic scenes of clifftop castles and rocky coasts and blasted branches growing out of roofs and battlements.

Towards the end of the eighteenth century the castle began to fall into disrepair. Early last century even the contents were sold, the Great Hall was used for a time as a granary for the home farm, and the building crumbled steadily into decay. Then Professor James Lorimer of Edinburgh University leased it as his summer residence.

One of his daughters has left a graphic description of the castle as she first knew it. Recalling that it was near-ruinous, she wrote: "It was left to the rooks and the owls, who built in its crumbling chimneys and dropped down piles of twigs which reached far into the rooms. Great holes let the rain and snow through the roofs, many of the floors had

[64]

Coat of arms, Kellie Castle.

become unsafe, every pane of glass was broken, and swallows built in the coronets on the ceilings, while the ceilings themselves sagged and in some cases fell into the rooms."

It was the Lorimers who in the past century saved the castle from ruin. Of the professor's two sons the elder was an artist, while the younger was Sir Robert Lorimer, designer of the Scottish National War Memorial and of the Thistle Chapel in St Giles Cathedral. Sir Robert's son, the sculptor Hew Lorimer, bought the castle in 1948 and major repairs were then carried out. Recently it was acquired by the National Trust for Scotland and in one room an Exhibition is featured in memory of Sir Robert. He was a pioneer in preserving Scotland's architectural heritage.

Today the Tolbooth bell hangs at the entrance to the Fisheries Museum.

6

Anster
and
Its
Caller
Herrin'

ONLY A MILE north of Pittenweem we
reach another of those East Neuk towns,
one with a name that makes places in
Wales like Llanvihangel-tor-ye-mynydd
and Llanfair-pwllgwngyll seem almost
indecently abrupt. You are now on the
outskirts of what is called in official
circles "the Royal Burgh of Kilrenny,
Anstruther Easter, and Anstruther
Wester".

The inhabitants, of course, don't use
that 58-letter name. They go to the
other extreme. In Anstruther Wester,
being individualists, they cut it down to
the six-letter word Anster and direct you
across the Dreel Burn if you are looking
for Anster Easter. But once you are
across the Dreel Burn, you will find that
Anster Easter doesn't exist. You are in
Anster now. You will have to go back
across the burn if you want to find
Anster Wester. If it all seems slightly
confusing at first, the important thing to
remember is that only incomers pro-
nounce Anster as Anster. The correct
way, by time-honoured usage, is 'Enster',
with the accent on the first 'e'.

The Kilrenny folk, up on their hilltop,
remain aloof from all this confusion.
After almost half-a-century of the official
union, they still belong to Kilrenny.
Which is fairly good proof that, in spite
of the planners, Fife will go on in its own
sweet way for ever.

This ancient ship is on a stone in Kilrenny churchyard.

Each of the East Neuk towns has an individuality of its own. St Monans is the slightly spooky one, Pittenweem the bewitching one, Crail the aristocratic one, and Anster is the homely one with atmosphere all round its shoulders and its feet planted firmly on the ground. One of the busiest shops along the shore is the ship chandler's. Another, nearby, stocks old-fashioned clay pipes. The price has gone up, over the years, from a penny in old money to 45 new pence for short-stemmed pipes and £1.20 for the long stemmed variety, but they still meet a ready sale. And until recent times, a barber in Shore Street had the traditional striped pole angled over his door, on the building that has its gutters halfway up the dormer windows, in the old Scottish style. A more modern version of the striped pole, flush against the building, has replaced it.

Shore Street has changed greatly. It used to be fringed with golden sands, when the sea trade was at its height, and ships lay with their long jib-booms close to the windows of the houses. But there was a quay as well, farther on. Baltic brigs and French wine ships used to lie there, three tiers deep, in the busy years of the 1730s.

You can still see the homes of some of the old sea captains and their families. Two captains lived next door to each other, beside the Dreel Burn in Castle Street. There was James Small of the "Good Design", who sailed from Anster in the mid-seventeenth century. He lived at 2 Castle Street. His son-in-law, his grandson and his great-grandson all became shipmasters like him. Next door at No. 3 was John Anstruther, a kinsman of the laird, and adventure was in his blood, for he became a Jacobite privateer with a very special mission. He collected his victims' arms and ammunition to equip the Royalist army of the Marquis of Montrose. This John Anstruther had a son who also became a privateer and is said to have grown

Jawbone of the biggest whale ever caught in Arctic waters became an archway.

This centre of fishing for six centuries is now the Scottish Fisheries Museum.

Exhibits in the Fisheries Museum are lively and comprehensive.

rich over the years, on the booty he got from capturing between sixty and seventy Dutch merchantmen.

Today there are reminders all around of those seafaring days. Up in Kilrenny, at the back of the church, is a gravestone on which some local sculptor carved a sturdy merchant ship three centuries ago. And in Anster Easter and Anster Wester are many carved stones to the memory of old-time shipmasters and merchants.

It was not only to the Low Countries and Scandinavia that the ships of Anster sailed. One July day in 1757 the "Rising Sun" arrived home, towing behind her a great whale from the coast of Greenland. It ended its days in the boiler-house, in the old fort at the end of Castle Street. In 1830, too, there was

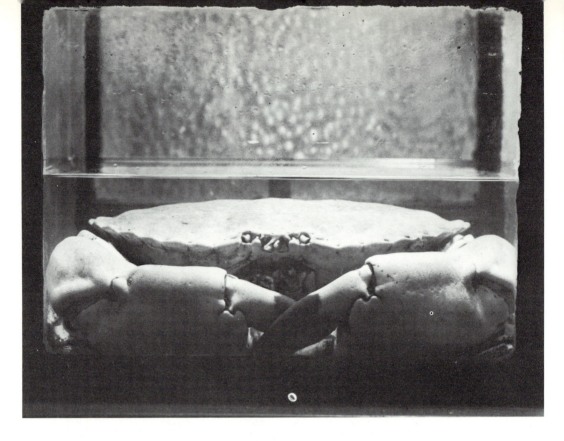

The partan who would not be stopped.

another reminder of Arctic voyagings. That year William Smith, who had been sailing with the Leith fleet, brought back to his home in Cellardyke the jawbone of the biggest whale that had ever been caught in the Arctic. He set it up at the back of his house, as an archway facing East Forth Street, and there it has remained ever since. In 1972 there was a solemn dedication ceremony, when a plaque was erected beside the jawbone, to spur on the youth of today to similar high endeavour. But William Smith did not just slaughter whales. He was an explorer, too. A sea passage leading to the North Pole is still called Smith Sound after him.

As in all the East Neuk towns, some houses in Anster are specially worth seeing. The Scottish Fisheries Museum at the head of the old quay is one of these. It stands on the site of a pre-Reformation chapel. And, though all that survives of this St Ayles Chapel is one arched window-head, you can still see beside it the early sixteenth century

building where the Abbot of Balmerino stayed on his visits. Today the site has entered on a new and much more exciting stage in its history. For those who know about fishing, it contains a vast amount of interesting material. And those who don't can learn about it in the most fascinating of all ways, with a fisherman as guide.

Here you can see the log books used by William Smith—the one who brought the giant whale's jawbone home to Cellardyke. As captain of the "Caledonia", in 1834, he didn't enter the number of whales he caught each day in the Davis Strait off the Greenland coast. Instead, very neatly, he marked each kill by drawing in the margin of his log book a silhouette of a whale's tail. One Sabbath he had to draw five of those silhouettes.

The old bell at the entrance originally hung in the Tolbooth from 1668 until 1872 when the building was demolished. A hundred years later, the bell was restored and put in its present position.

A genuine set of home-made oil-skins, with adhering fish scales.

A private pend off Shore Street, Anster.

The inscription reads: "Anstruther Easter—Recte faciendo neminem timas" (Do right and fear no one). But the museum deals not only with the past. It has brought the story of the sea up to date with a memorial to Scottish fishermen lost at sea. All who died prior to 1946 are noted in a book of remembrance, while those lost since that date are named on brass plaques.

The museum contains a fascinating collection of model fishing boats, fishing gear and equipment, maps and compasses. Fishermen's clothes are modelled on life-size figures. One of these outfits dating from 1870, had been discovered during the repair of a roof. It still had herring scales adhering to the oilskin trousers, an old type with leather seat for wear when rowing, and known locally as "brooks". These were made by the fisher folk themselves.

And fish, too, have invaded the museum. In large wall tanks you can get a close-up view of the deadly conger eel, as well as more palatable fish. And in a floor pool, with a surrounding wall, you can see three varieties of crab including the partan, the only edible one of the three. Thereby hangs a tale. A fisherman of Crail gifted a huge partan, about five pounds in weight, for display in the aquarium. But its homing instinct was too highly developed. Twice it climbed out of the water and up the wall, to fall head-first down on the outside. The first time it was safely returned to the pool. The second time it was killed by the fall. You can still see this giant wanderer, preserved in his own small tank, beside the pool.

Nearby, at the back of the pend at 41-43 Shore Street, is a massive staircase tower supported by heavy corbelling and with a little iron-barred window close to the top. Here again is a reminder that East Neuk folk liked to be different. You will not find a staircase tower like

In Anster, a staircase tower with corbelled support.

Buckie House has been a showplace in Anster Wester for over a hundred years.

This attractive home was long ago a popular inn.

it, anywhere around, even in a castle.

There is a rather special flavour of the sea about a couple of buildings farther west, one in Anster Easter and the other in Anster Wester. They stand on each side of the bridge which crosses the Dreel Burn and both are decorated with sea-shells. The one in Anster Wester, a three-storeyed house built by a seventeenth century merchant, is known as Buckie House. Last century it was occupied by Alexander Batchelor, an eccentric slater, who provided the shell decorations.

Though the outside in his day was delightful, that was merely a foretaste of the greater wonders inside. He attracted visitors with a notice:

> Here is the famous Grotto Room,
> The like's not seen in any toun;
> Those who do it wish to see,
> It's only threepence asked as fee.

So you went upstairs to the Grotto Room, which really was special. The entire ceiling and window embrasures were most beautifully decorated with East Neuk shells in a colour scheme of cream and brown. Not only has it survived the years undamaged. Even the rich colouring is now restored to its original brightness.

That, however, was merely the setting. For the focal point of his whole design you had to turn to a little alcove near the door of this upstairs room. Folk say that Batchelor had to search every beach on the twenty-mile stretch of coastline between Fife Ness and Lower Largo, on his hands and knees, to find the beautiful little John o' Groats shells which cover this most special treasure. It became the real showpiece. For a payment of threepence he would pose in it for you and for an extra penny you could step inside yourself and have the lid closed on you. But now the alcove is empty. When Alex. Batchelor died in the spring of 1863 he was buried in this shell-covered coffin.

Just across the road is the Esplanade and at No. 3 is one of the finest moulded doorways in the whole East Neuk. It was erected more than two and a half

The moulded doorway at 3 The Esplanade, Anster Wester.

Little in Anster Wester predates this church building.

From the old Tolbooth jail.

centuries ago, in 1718. But that is not so very old for these parts. The tower of the church across the road is two centuries older. And it has seen stirring times. A drunken sergeant from Cromwell's army burst the door open one day and threw the pulpit Bible into the river. A century earlier a couple of English pirates were brought all the way from Suffolk to be hanged at the end of the Esplanade, close to the churchyard. Here, too, last century, a housewife watched the Resurrectionists in the churchyard throwing their stolen corpse into a boat in the burn.

At that time Anstruther Easter Church had a rather formidable beadle called Thomas Barclay and when he learned about these dreadful goings-on in the Wester Churchyard he was heard to remark "Weel, Ah tell ye this, there's no' a livin' soul will be taken oot o' my kirkyaird!"

All the traffic along the coast used this Esplanade in bygone days, for it led—as it still does — to the Stepping Stones across the Dreel Burn. These were used for hundreds of years before the bridge was built.

King James V, who loved to roam the countryside getting to know his people, arrived here one day disguised as a piper. The river was running high and the steps were submerged. But a beggar's wife recognised him and, kilting her

Not unusual in the East Neuk.

coats, carried him across on her shoulder to the other side. Out of that story was born a famous club of the eighteenth century—the Beggars' Benison.

Forming clubs was a popular pastime among the landed gentry of those days. The Society of St Andrews Golfers was formed in 1754, to enjoy the golf and good company after. Dinner clubs were popular too, in Edinburgh and elsewhere. But this Anstruther club, with branches later in Edinburgh and in London, was among the most famous of them all. Founded in 1730 it was not only one of the earliest. It was very different from the others too.

There were thirty-two members of this most puissant and honourable order of the Beggars' Benison—among them the Earl of Kellie (better known as "Fiddler Tam"), Lord Newark and several lairds of lang pedigree. They met in what soon became a notorious howff in the Card's Wynd, just south of Anster Easter churchyard. The proceedings began with the re-enactment of the royal crossing of the Dreel Burn and that got them in the mood for the livelier scenes ahead. Once a year, in November, they had their collar day, when they wore their medals and the knight-companions elected their sovereign for the ensuing year. It is said that the Prince Regent, afterwards George IV, was thrilled beyond expression when he was enthroned as sovereign of the London branch.

The stepping stones across The Dreel Burn, where the Beggars' Benison began.

The Beggars' Benison.

But all good things must come to an end. The Beggars' Benison met no more after 1836 and eventually its remaining funds were used to provide an annual prize in the burgh school. Only the memory was left. One writer last century remembered: "About sixty years ago Anster had the reputation of being the most drunken town on the coast. How else could it be, with the Beggars' Benison and other social clubs patronised by the first in the land?" Even the Scottish National Museum of Antiquities remembers. There the club medal and its moulds are displayed in a showcase, with a little notice recalling that this was a club of rakes, with vice, gambling and the bottle their main pursuits.

Anster's seafaring days were already passing when that club was formed, but by the second half of the eighteenth century a thriving fishing industry had sprung up in Anster Easter and neighbouring Kilrenny. Weavers for most of the year, they left their looms in early summer and went down the hill to bring out their fishing gear from the cellars where they had stored it under the dyke. And off they sailed from Cellardyke to Peterhead and Wick for the "Lammas Drave", the summer herring fishing.

Eventually, when the demand for hand-loom weaving died out, they combined their fishing with part-time crofting. Then they became fishermen all the time, with winter days spent out beyond the Isle of May at the white fishing. That brought changes, for the cadgers arrived to buy the catch and this "set of loud-voiced fellows galloped away with their cart-loads of fish into the quiet villages of Fife, their big blue bonnets pulled belligerently down the nape of their neck—ready for anything, from selling a herring to engaging in a single combat with a customer who was inclined to haggle a little about the price." It brought a new liveliness into those inland villages—as well as a taste for fish.

The Dreel Castle guards only Castle Street today.

Though the weavers are gone, their cottages at Kilrenny are as trim as ever.

By the middle of last century, with big herring shoals in the Firth of Forth, Anstruther was fast becoming Scotland's principal fishing port. Well over 700 men and boys were going out with the fleet and twice as many folk were employed on shore, making the nets and barrels, gutting, curing, and packing. There were great stacks of herring barrels piled high on the quayside. "I've lived to see seven to nine thousand coopered in a single day at the pier," said one retired fisherman. He was not exaggerating. Well over a thousand people were gutting and packing at the busiest time of the year. And still the number of local boats was growing, until soon there were well over two hundred.

It was not only in the herring season that the pressure was on. Early in January 1869 the local curers set up a new record, when a fleet of over forty boats arrived home from a day's fishing with a catch of fifty tons of haddock. The entire catch was smoked and sent off by train in time to be served for high tea in Glasgow the following night.

By the 1880's the trade was at its height. "If you would see life in earnest," said one writer then, "come in spring when a hundred wagons will dash away by nightfall with 'caller herrin, new drawn frae the firth,' to every city and market town in merrie England." Anstruther had no equal in Scotland.

There were then almost a thousand boats in its fishing fleet and over six hundred of these were in the first class, used with net as well as line. Even the crab and lobster fishers had 116 yawls. And though the value of money was infinitely higher than now, this fleet with its nets and lines was estimated even by the standards of those days to be worth more than a fifth of a million pounds. The number of fishermen had reached almost 4000. They provided work for eighty coopers and 47 fish curers—"and 2362 fair sisters who waken the echoes with joyous song as they ply knife and spit, etc., in the fish-yard."

The lasses were busy at one thing or another, all along the East Neuk coast—

The lasses o' the Ferry
  They busk braw;
The lasses o' the Elie,
  They ding a';
The lasses o' St Monan,
  They curse and ban;
The lasses o' Pittenweem,
  They do the same;
The lasses o' Anster,
  They drink strong ale;
There's green grass in Cellardyke
  And crabs in till Crail.

By that time the statisticians had discovered that the Anstruther fishing was providing work for no fewer than 6386 people. And though it went as it had come, when the herring shoals moved elsewhere, Anster has continued

How to get over the sea wall.

through the years to hold its place as the very hub of life in the East Neuk.

There still remains a souvenir of the earliest days of the fishing boom, when the weavers of Kilrenny used to sail away to the Lammas Drave. Some of their cottages have survived. They can be seen not far from the Church, in Prospect Row, restored and as pretty as a picture. There were weavers in those cottages as late as the 1830's — members of the Weavers' Society of Kilrenny. They had a charity box — a brabners' box — for those who needed a helping hand when times were hard. But a windfall of £80 went to their heads and soon the box was empty. "It was the unexpected legacy that did it," said one of them ruefully. "Some of us couldna, wouldna rest till we killed the goose wi' the golden egg."

Weavers no longer live in those cottages. Long ago they moved down the hill to Cellardyke, where they planted their clothes poles along the shore as an Empire-builder would plant his flag. Clothes lines by the sea-shore or in a fisherman's yard, or outside his cottage in the wynd where he lives, are like the registered coat-of-arms of his profession. He has changed his fishing methods. His boats too are bigger and safer and infinitely better equipped. And he lives in a much more comfortable house.

The old days of the smoke-begrimed but-and-ben, with unplastered walls and an earthen floor and the big double bed in a murky recess are gone for ever. But still his womenfolk have their washing endlessly bleaching on the line, in Cellardyke and all the other fishtowns along the East Neuk.

It is not just that the men arrive home soaked to the skin, sometimes bringing back more wet clothes than fish. That may have started the habit but there is more to it than that. The women will tell you that for whiteness — for pure whiteness instead of blue whiteness — they wouldn't change the salt air at the shore for a boatload of modern detergents. But the older men will tell you that the poles were put there originally for quite a different purpose. That was where their fathers and grandfathers used to spread their nets.

Washing is still hung out beside the sea wall at Cellardyke.

The Manse, Kilrenny.

7

The Oldest Manse in Scotland

WE HAVE, of course, forgotten one or two things about Anster. We haven't mentioned its most famous building or its most notable inhabitant or even its most exciting times. So let us pick up the threads. All these are connected with a house high on the hill overlooking the sea—the oldest manse in Scotland. It was built almost four hundred years ago.

Its builder was James Melville, whom we shall meet later as a student at St Andrews University. He was the boy who arrived at St Andrews with his glub and bals, after learning to play goff at a school near Montrose; he was the University student who upset the rest of the class, when he grat all through the lessons until the Regent gave him private tuition; and he was the one who so graphically described the aged John Knox almost flying out of the pulpit in the vehemence of his preaching.

In his early twenties James returned, as also had his fiery uncle Andrew Melville, to the University as a lecturer at St Mary's College. James was a remarkable scholar. He had just come from Glasgow University, where he taught Greek, Logic, Rhetoric, Mathematics and Natural Philosophy. And now he was Professor of Hebrew and Oriental Languages at St Andrews. The only trouble was that, with a young wife and a growing family he was earning too little to keep them all. The prospects were much better as a minister. So, in the summer of 1586, he moved to Anster Wester, to a house which has long since disappeared, to become minister of all the coastal strip from Abercrombie to Kilrenny.

He had just arrived when drama struck his parish and the best of the able-bodied men, armed to the teeth, went sailing off to sea. English pirates were the cause of the trouble. Off the East Neuk they pillaged a barque that was sailing home to Anster and killed one of the crew. Then they invaded the roadstead of Pittenweem, boarded another vessel and, beating up its crew in full view of the townspeople, sailed off with plunder from it as well. An insult so gross could not be ignored. The men of Anster armed their fastest ship, picked their best seamen and fighters, and set off in pursuit.

The new minister was all against it. To him the little finger of the least valiant of his flock was worth a whole shipload of pirates. For almost nine days he neither ate nor drank and seldom closed his eyes. But then the ships returned, with flags and streamers flying, and they all went joyfully into the kirk at Anster Wester and praised God, before hanging two of the pirates at the pier-end, beside the Dreel Burn. After that there was time to hear what

had happened. Soon after leaving Anster, the avengers met a warship from St Andrews that was fast and powerfully armed and only too pleased to drop everything else and join in such a necessary venture. This mighty ship led the way impressively, stopping all the vessels it met and forcing them to pay homage to the King of Scotland. One proud, stiff Englishman refused to do reverence and with the first cannon-ball his mainsail was down.

They sailed as far as the Suffolk coast and then they sighted their quarry, busy again plundering a ship from Anster. The pirates scurried ashore, with the Scots in hot pursuit, and soon half-a-dozen men were taken prisoners. The whole countryside was roused by the uproar. But it all ended happily when the Justices of the Peace, having heard the facts, yielded like the shipmasters along the route and did reverence to the King of Scotland. So the prisoners were shared out—two to be hanged at Anster and the other four at St Andrews. After that James Melville was able to get on with his preaching.

For two years life jogged along quietly for the new minister, but by the summer of 1588 the whole coastline suddenly became agog with rumours. The Armada had sailed from Spain. Already it had reached the East Coast and was moving steadily north. Its commanders were

At the pier-end, where they hanged the pirates.

planning to land and join the Papists, to turn Scotland into a Catholic country again. There had been a landing at Dunbar—or was it near the mouth of the Tay or at Aberdeen or Cromarty?

One by one the rumours were proved wrong. And then, three months later, Melville was roused from his sleep at dawn one day, to find an Anster bailie standing at his bedside. "I haiff to tell you newes, Sir," he told the still drowsy minister. And news he certainly had. A Spanish galleon with a crew of 260 men had sailed into the harbour over-night and tied up at the quayside. There had been no fighting. The commander wanted to meet someone who could speak Spanish or some other mutual language, and the bailie came to the manse because Melville — with his knowledge of Greek and Rhetoric, Mathematics and Oriental Languages—

happened also to be the only person in Anster able to understand what the Spaniard had to say.

So he met Don Jan de Gomez de Medina, squadron commander of twenty galleons. And though this Spanish grandee had brought four of his captains with him, he came in peace. There was good reason for that. All the rest of his squadron was lying wrecked at Fair-Isle and he wanted the King's help to get back to Spain with his men.

Eventually Jan de Gomez and his captain were housed by the laird in his castle, while the crew were barracked in the town and fed on a rather spartan diet of kail, porridge and fish. But there was no restriction on their movement and they went freely about the town. People felt rather sorry for the crew. They were merely beardless youths, look-ing "sillie, trauchled and houngered".

[93]

Most of their time they were going from house to house, begging for more food. As for the commander and his captains, they were the soul of courtesy, bowing low to every seaman they met in the street. There had never been a sight like this in Anster before.

When they returned to Spain there was a happy sequel. Jan de Gomez discovered that an Anster ship was lying in a Spanish port under arrest. Engineering an audience with the King, he described the kindly welcome he had received in Scotland and persuaded him to release the ship. After entertaining the crew at his palatial mansion he sent them home with his kindest regards to the laird and the minister. But Melville still kept thanking God that they had not landed three months earlier.

A shadow had fallen over the manse by then, for the minister's infant son Andrew had been failing for weeks and was only too obviously dying. Somewhere the sorrowing father had read that in Ancient Egypt, at a time like that, they used to hang up a picture of Death and looking at it helped to soften the final blow. He had no suitable picture but he set up the child at the end of the table, at dinner-time and supper-time, in the hope that this would do instead. It didn't. The end came just as harshly as he had feared. And an odd thing happened. He had two white pigeons that he kept in the manse and one of these wouldn't stay out of the cradle on the day of the baby's death. They died almost simultaneously in the cradle together. And the other pigeon, after whimpering endlessly, was also dead within three hours.

*   *   *

By 1589 Melville was looking for other ministers for Abercrombie, Pittenweem and Anstruther Wester, and had decided to take charge of Kilrenny alone. It had neither a manse nor a glebe. But that was soon remedied. As he pointed out in his Diary, God quickly moved the people to build him a house, on a piece of land that the Laird of Anstruther gifted. The only trouble was that He didn't move them quite enough.

In June 1590 the work on the manse began — not beside the church at Kilrenny but on the hill above Anster Easter which was then a part of Kilrenny parish. Soon the materials were arriving at the site. Day after day the stones, a gift from the people of Anster, were dragged up the hill on sledges. Three thousand sledge-loads were brought altogether. And the landward members of the congregation, not to be outdone, supplied vast quantities of lime. About fifteen tons of it were brought in the panniers of ponies. But, in spite of all that, the minister had to admit it was not enough. If God had

The vaulted cellar restored.

The Spanish paychest above the door.

not made him take over the work himself, and provided him with all the rest of the materials he needed, the manse would never have been finished. He had set his heart not on a manse of three thousand stones but of six thousand, and that meant twice as much lime as well.

It was no ordinary manse. Melville was descended from a line of lairds, and he built his home like a castle, with cellar doors of nail-studded oak and walls so massive that he had one stair leading straight up in the thickness of the wall, from the barrel-vaulted kitchen to the dining room above. The house even looked like a castle. Today it is T-shaped only because a west wing was added in 1650. In his day it was L-shaped like many a castle, with the entrance doorway safe from attack, in the re-entrant angle. Two barrel-vaulted storage cellars along with the kitchen occupied the ground floor, with the public rooms above and the bedrooms still higher. And right on top, with a glorious view, was his study. He never called his manse a castle. High on the gable outside his little study he put a plaque with the words "THE WATCH TOWR" for all to read. But even in castles this part of the building was often called the watch tower.

In the garden he had a brewhouse, a doocot for his pigeons and a kitchen midden nearer the house. All trace of the brewhouse has vanished but the doocot is still there and so was the kitchen midden within living memory.

Nine months after he started to build his manse, he was able to move in. Everything had gone smoothly. There had been not a single accident — not even a finger hurt. And every week he was able to pay the workmen their wages in full. But now the day of reckoning had come. The cost had been 3500 marks, about nine times his annual stipend. He was left so heavily in debt that he was sorely tempted to give it all up and go off to some church elsewhere. There were tempting offers too — from St Giles Cathedral, Edinburgh, St Mary's, Dundee, and St Andrews. But

James Melville's "Watch Towr".

sermons and writing his Diary and praying and weeping for his congregation, and pondering over affairs of state. For he was no ordinary parish minister. Even before he built his manse he was one of the leading figures in the General Assembly, the only one to whom King James VI was willing to listen with any genuine patience. "My wisest and gravest counsellor," he called him.

All the evidence indicates that Melville was a gentle man, full of humanity and with infinite tact. They were rare qualities in a minister in those days. The King, who knew him well, often sought his advice on church matters, until one day things went wrong.

It was in 1596 that the trouble exploded. Among the ministers of the church the wreck of the Armada had not brought an end to worries about a Catholic coup. At the General Assembly they were obsessed with the idea that plots were hatching. And when they were not worrying about Catholics, they were very worried about Bishops. The King had an unfortunate habit of not sharing their worries on either point and one day in 1596 he allowed two of his great Catholic Lords—Errol and Huntly —to return to Scotland from exile. The General Assembly was firmly convinced that those two Lords were the key figures in a Papist plot to overthrow the new and true religion. They were

he avoided the temptation. And the next year he was given an unexpected increase in his stipend. "It is a good thing to give to God," he records in his diary, "for He will repay you twice as much as you give Him. And yet, what can we give to God? It is all His own already!"

The manse has had its share of drama over the years. In the study there was said to be a second floor hidden beneath the one you see—a fact confirmed during the 1977 restoration of the manse—with a trap door leading to a secret stair, and this takes you down to an underground escape route that leads to St Andrews Road.

The carved panel above the study door came from the flagship of the Spanish Armada, and was indeed part of the Admiral's paychest, presented to Melville as a keepsake by Jan de Gomez. And on the wall without a window is a curious recess where he is said to have kept the few books he possessed. The little fireplace, too, with its moulded surround was familiar to him. Night after night he sat in front of it, preparing his

*A gruesome murder
is the theme of this
plaster cast.*

wrong but they appointed a deputation to see the King and tell him what a dreadful mistake he had made. The fiery Andrew Melville, the acknowledged leader of them all, and uncle to the gentle James, had to be in the deputation. And since he was sure to lose his temper within the first five minutes, James had to be in it too, as a more tactful spokesman for them all.

So they set off across Fife to royal Falkland Palace. Having passed through the great gate between the twin towers, they were led up the wide turnpike stair into a long hall, where armed guards were walking to and fro, and watching their every move. They reached the far end of the hall and were ushered into the handsomely furnished Presence Chamber beyond. Fine tapestries hung on its walls and the royal chair with its silken fringe was richly covered with velvet. At

[98]

the end of the chamber, a door led into the King's private dining room. On the right, another was to his bedroom. And the bedroom still exists, restored to look very much as he must have known it. But the dining-room is no longer there or the outer hall with its guards. And all that remains of the Presence Chamber is one roofless wall, overlooking the inner courtyard. Falkland, like most old castles and palaces, has fared less happily than the minister's manse at Kilrenny.

That day in 1596 King James was not very glad to see the deputation. Even though James Melville used that "myld and smothe maner quhilk the King lyked best of", His Majesty still refused to believe there was any Papist threat. So he crabbedly interrupted the Anstruther minister in the middle of his message from the General Assembly. That started the fiery Andrew off. Soon the King and he were shouting at the top of their voices, and since Andrew had the louder voice his words carried best. With a cry that sounded like the crack of doom he told King James that he was no more than "God's sillie vassal".

Then, grasping the King's sleeve, he roared: "And thairfor, Sir, I mon tell you thair is twa Kings and twa King-domes in Scotland. Thair is Chryst Jesus the King, and his kingdome the Kirk, whase subject King James the Saxt is, and of whase kingdome nocht a king, nor a lord, nor a heid, bot a member!"

It was not exactly news to the King. He had not forgotten that, of seven Stuart sovereigns who preceded him, six had met violent deaths. And so, perhaps better than Andrew Melville himself, he realised that sovereigns were not immortal. But Andrew's clarion call at least sounded loud. Soon all the rest of the ministers knew what he had told the King and were mightily fortified. James VI did not forget either. From then on, he drifted steadily apart from his Presbyterian ministers. Next year he deposed Andrew from the Rectorship of St Andrews University and within a few more years he had him a prisoner in the Tower of London. James Melville, too, was severed from his own congregation in the last few years of his life. In 1607 he was warded in Newcastle, and still in exile he died at Berwick in 1614. His will showed that he was a man of considerable wealth, with a bed and mattress worth twice as much as his library of books.

If the people of Anstruther thought the manse was theirs, they were doomed to disappointment. When James Melville made up his will, he forgot about the stones from Anster and the lime from the country folk, and the site being gifted by the laird, and how much he had once felt beholden to God for the rest. He regarded the manse as his own and left it to his son. It remained in his family until 1637 when it was sold by his grandson Ephraim to Sir William Anstruther, who added a west wing to the house. For the next eighty years it was occupied mostly by the ladies of the Anstruther family in their widowhood. One of them, Lady Melrose, committed suicide in the little study which Melville had known so well and the ghost of the Green Lady began to haunt the manse.

Archbishop Sharp of St Andrews knew the house too. Indeed he spent the last night of his life there in May, 1679. He had come from Edinburgh, landing by boat at Lower Largo and travelling along the coast to Anstruther to confer with Sir William, and the next day, in his coach, he took the inland

The minister drew baptismal water from the Manse's garden well.

route with one of his daughters. At
Ceres he smoked a pipe with the curate
and then he drove on over the cobbled
bridge of Ceres, on the old main road
to St Andrews. And on Magus Muir he
was murdered.

In the Manse the Anstruthers put up
a souvenir of his death. On the magnificent memorial which the Archbishop's
son erected in the parish church at St
Andrews, one marble tablet shows the
actual murder scene on Magus Muir.
The Anstruthers obtained a plaster cast
of this and kept it in their tower house.
And there it could be seen until 1718,
when the house became a manse again
—for a new Presbyterian minister, the
Rev. James Nairn. After that the plaster
cast was banished out of sight and out
of mind, into a corner of one of the
barrel-vaulted cellars. And there it
remained until 1914 when another
minister of Anstruther discovered it
buried under a mountain of coal dross
in the cellar and had it cleaned and
restored to a more honoured place in the
recess where Melville is thought to have
kept his books in his Watch Tower
study.

Just before James Nairn became
minister the Kirk Session of Anstruther
had regained possession of the Melville
Manse by effecting an exchange with Sir
William Anstruther for other property
which they owned, but shortly after this
agreement was entered into the elders

found that they had got a bad bargain (or maybe vandals had been busy during the time of the hand over!) At any rate the building was in a sorry state of repair. Many of the windows had been broken and even the wooden frames removed and there were as many of the big grey Angus slates on the ground around the manse as on the roof itself. An architect was brought in to find whether repair was possible. His feet went though the floorboards, landing him with a painful bump astride one of the beams.

After reading his report, some thought the only sensible way was to demolish the building and erect a new one. A new manse was to cost £190 and the repairs—it was thought— only £120. So the old manse was restored and, for the first time in its long history, the walls were lathed and plastered. The estimate, however, was not quite accurate. Years later the minister of those days recalled that over the years "he had spent mair oot o' his ain pouch than wud hae rebuilt it".

Yet another chapter opened for James Melville's old manse in 1977 when three years of renovation work was completed under the leadership of the Reverend Charles W. Miller and his Kirk Session, with generous assistance from the Historic Buildings Council for Scotland and the Pilgrim and Russell Trusts.

Uncovering blocked-up windows and doorways long hidden from view and incorporating the stone barrel-vaulted cellars, they created a 20th century home within the 16th century walls. This was all so excellently executed that the Saltire Society of Scotland selected it for one of their major awards of that year, with yet another award being given to the craftsmen (all Anstruther men, as in Melville's day) for "the high standard of the work done".

* * *

During happier times for the Melvilles King James gave the Minister of Kilrenny the Royal Charter for Anster Easter, where it has remained ever since.

The King wrote: We greet you well, seeing that you seek the election of the town of Anstruther as a royal burgh, this has now been confirmed in our late Parliament held at Linlithgow, and now in our perfect age, continuing in like goodwill towards the inhabitants thereof, that the welfare of the said burgh may increase, it is our will and deliberate mind that this be now confirmed in the present parliament without any limitation. I charge you therefore that ye hold hand to the same, to the effect that none of the liberties or privileges pertaining to the said burgh be in any sort impaired by their presence. Subscribed with our hand at Holyrood House the 11th day of July, 1587.   JAMES R.

The Royal Charter of the town.

Crail had its share—and more—of Fife's early adventuring.

8

Crail
the
Magnificent

NOW LET us move further north to Crail, the most ancient and splendid of the East Neuk burghs. It still has an indefinable air of well-being and all the panoply of its historic past. Centuries ago its rich merchants built their handsome houses round its market place, and there is scarcely another town in Europe with a market place so spacious. Near one end is the Tolbooth with an 18th century belfry on top of a building that has been there since the 16th century. The unusual ogee roof of the belfry is sometimes thought to have been inspired by those that the merchants saw on their travels in the Low Countries. But roofs like this were not so very uncommon in Scotland then. The bell in the belfry was cast in Holland in 1520.

At the other end of the Marketgate is the Church of St Mary, far more ancient than the Tolbooth. The tower, the nave, with its red sandstone pillars and the chancel in its slightly later Gothic style were all built in the 13th century. And the actual origin of the church goes back even further to the mid-12th century, when Crail was already becoming a noted seaport.

It was a hazardous business building a church in those days. In St Andrews, St Rule's Tower became the object of a giant's wrath. The church at Crail offended an even more powerful person-

The Blue Stone still bears the Devil's mark.

A battlemented mort house guarded Crail's dead from the robbers.

A Nethergate miniature.

age in the Devil himself, who was in residence on the Isle of May at the time. He hurled a great boulder at the church as they built it. And though the island was five-and-a-half miles distant and the boulder split as it flew through the air, one part did in fact land at the eastern end of the market place, only thirty yards from the churchyard gate.

You can still see a hollow in the stone, where the burghers of Crail used to sharpen their spears and arrows before setting off for battle. They thought this Devil's stone beside the church would bring them safely home. But there was already a hollow before the burghers began to deepen it. That is the Devil's thumb print, where he grasped the stone as he threw it. The other part — the bigger one—landed on Balcomie Sands. And it too has the thumb mark, showing that he used a two-handed grip.

If the old parish church had its troubles at the start, it had them again a century and a half ago. Those were the days when medical research was growing fast. And some people were only too willing to unearth the dead, within hours of their interment. To get bodies for dissecting in those days was as hard as getting hearts and lungs today.

The East Neuk has many a tale of

The beehive doocot is seldom seen outside of Fife.

The old spelling was Marketgait, meaning Market Street.

those body-snatchers. It is said that one venerable minister was buried beside the gable of his village church and only a gaping hole was there next morning. There was a housewife too at Anstruther, whose home overlooked the churchyard. Roused by a muffled noise in the night, she looked out to see a body being pushed into a sack and the sack thrown into a boat in the Dreel Burn. There was a student too, who spent a long summer holiday in the East Neuk. He was such a cheery companion and so full of tricks that everyone liked him. When eventually he took the stage-coach home, quite a few of his new friends came along to the inn to wave good-bye. He died soon after of gunshot wounds in the churchyard of another town in Fife.

And there was John Ramsay in Kilrenny, who lived all his life on the charity of neighbours. It was only when he died in the 1820s that they discovered he possessed a fortune. He made a will in which he stated: "I am to be buried as near as may be to my mother on the sunny side of Kilrenny Kirk, under a big red stone, ten feet deep, to keep my body from the inhuman monsters —the Resurrection men." In Crail the risks were just as great. There, at a corner of the churchyard, they built a square mort house with gunloops and battlements, where they stored their dead until danger was past. And on it they

In honour of the Crail capon.

put an inscribed tablet: "Erected for securing the dead, 1826."

Midway between the church and the tolbooth, in the great market place, is the market cross, the symbol that this was a royal burgh with vast trading privileges. No single cross could last all the years of a burgh as old as Crail, and the present one with its unicorn on top is modern. But a very similar one, no doubt, looked down in bygone days on Crail's historic Sunday markets. It was in 1310 that King Robert the Bruce granted the burghers the right to hold those markets on the Sabbath day and for many years after the Reformation the burghers defied all efforts by the General Assembly to change it to a week-day.

The Reformation changed many things in Crail. It was here, in 1559, that John Knox began his campaign to destroy the monasteries. And one that suffered was the nunnery down in the Nethergate. Its handsome precinct wall, then new built, has survived to modern times. But only a small fragment of the nunnery itself remains. The doocot, which provided a winter supply of pigeon meat, fared better than the nuns. It still stands, as solid as ever. It is circular — a style more common in Fife than anywhere else in Scotland.

It was not the religious buildings, the tolbooth or even the market place, however, which provided the real key to Crail's medieval prosperity. The most important place in this royal burgh was its harbour. And to reach the old harbour at Crail you can go down the Shoregate, the most picturesque of all the streets in this picturesque town. At the foot, overlooking the quay, is the 17th century Custom House with a pend at one end and a plaque above it showing a ship in the olden days. Up town

Shoregate, with its outside stairs, leads down to the old harbour at Crail.

Lobster creels lie sweetening alongside the boiler house at Crail.

A house decoration.

in the Nethergate is another plaque erected last century, of a schooner in full sail.

It was up and down the winding streets between the harbour and the Marketgate that life revolved in Crail from the 12th century on. For centuries its ships came back full laden with cargoes from the Low Countries and Scandinavia. But not all the men of Crail were merchants and seamen trading with the Continent. There were fishermen too. Ships from all over Northern Europe used to come to Crail for that special delicacy, the far-famed Crail capon.

Like the Bombay duck, the Crail capon had nothing to do with bird life. There is one on top of the weathervane on the Tolbooth steeple. But even by the time the steeple was built, in the eighteenth century, the trade was beginning to decline. The fishermen of Crail have forgotten about their capon. They might be able to tell you it was a haddock, but whether it was smoked or just dried they can no longer remember. The making of a Crail capon is one of the lost arts of Fife. It was almost certainly not smoked, however, for the trade in capons came to an end just when kippering was beginning to take the place of sun-drying.

But in Crail the fishermen have no complaints about this lost trade. They still catch the best crabs on the whole coast and many a good lobster too. That keeps them busy for most of the year, with the partan fishing coming to a height in the early spring. And after the crabs have gone creeping out to deeper water, the lobsters come to their best in the harvest time. The harbour wall is piled high with creels, sweetening in the wind and sunshine.

It is strange how names and customs differ among fishermen along the coast. On the Angus coast, at Arbroath, those creels are more commonly known as "sunks" and sometimes in Montrose as "lobster pots" though they bear no resemblance to a real one. Along the Angus coast too the creels are never seen in large numbers out airing. They are used with scarcely a break through the season. Farther north in the Mearns, which is famed like Crail for its lobsters, they talk of creels again and dip them in tarry "bark" and pile them up on the quayside. There they lie for a fortnight or more at Johnshaven. But at Crail,

[115]

after going through the boiler-house and getting their bark, they are left from April to October. Even if a creel had a smell about it you could still catch lobsters. It is all a question of the size of the catch. The fishermen of Crail will tell you that if they were less careful the catch just wouldn't come up to their expectations. Lobsters, like salmon, are fussy that way.

At times there is drama along the coast, when conger eels get among the young lobsters and crabs. Even the cod comes preying. But worst of all are the squids. They will actually invade a creel with a full-grown lobster inside, and suck it out until every trace of flesh has gone, with only the bare shell left behind.

If some lobsters die the hard way, so too do old superstitions among the fisherfolk, even in sophisticated Crail. At sea they don't mention the word pig and salmon they prefer to call red fish. But now they no longer run to hide, if a minister is glimpsed coming down towards the harbour. They leave that to the fishermen of other ports, farther along the East Neuk. The womenfolk too no longer think of a bouillabaisse of skate-brew as a remedy for a childless marriage, or even as a cordial to take the chill out of wedlock. The very phrase "Awa an' sup skate-bree!" is almost forgotten.

Forgotten too is the marvellous skate that was caught one day in the early 1800s. As soon as the fishermen started cutting it up, it leaped from the table and snapped and bit. It wounded several people, until they fled in all directions. At last an elder of the kirk collected a coffin and persuaded the rest to help him gather the pieces of this enormous skate. When that was done they buried it as close as they could to the churchyard wall. It had probably been feeding on some human body in the sea and "imbibed some of the nature and feeling of man". You can read all about it in "Travels in Scotland", which the Rev. James Hall wrote soon after. And a minister surely couldn't be wrong about that!

But though some of the old life of Crail is fast becoming forgotten, Crail itself is still the unforgettable. The harbour is now partly silted up and scarcely usable. But scores of artists, and photographers in their hundreds, come there. It is quite the most photographed place in all Fife.

The Harbour, Crail.

Once, long ago, there was a chapel building, out beyond the Long Pier.

9

St Andrews

Golf
and
Gown

THERE IS a mythical bird, the phoenix, that lives for five hundred years in the lonely wildernesses of the world. When it senses death approaching, it builds a funeral pyre and, setting it alight, plunges headlong into the flames. And out of the ashes of the dead bird a new one is born to live another five hundred years. It can go on for ever like that. One might say the same about St Andrews. It too once felt death approaching and out of the ruins of the old city a new one was born. You become conscious of that, as you walk through its streets. All around are reminders of its earlier existence, when not another town in Scotland could compare with it in the richness of life it offered to its citizens.

Its very name stirs up memories of Scotland's patron saint and the blue and white cross of its national flag. And these go back a long way, well over a thousand years, into the Dark Ages.

At that time a saintly monk called Rule was living in Patras, in Western Greece. One night, in a vision, he was told to travel far from his native land to the west. And so, with a priest, two deacons, eight hermits and three devout virgins for company, he sailed the length of the Mediterranean and round the coast of Spain and France, always looking for a sign from God. It came with unmistakable force, just after they had passed the East Neuk of Fife. In

The Prospect of the Town of St Andrews, by Captain John Slezer.

a violent storm their ship was wrecked in a bay and they scrambled ashore more dead than alive. But Rule was still clutching his most cherished possession, a box which contained a human arm-bone, three fingers from a right hand, one tooth and a kneecap, all genuine relics of St Andrew, who had been martyred in Rule's native town of Patras.

Even after the missionaries escaped from their watery grave, they were still not out of danger. The King of the Picts came down to the shore to see what he could plunder. To his amazement a great white cross appeared in the blue sky and the awe-struck King hurriedly turned Christian, for there was no sense in tempting Providence too far. That was how a white cross on a blue background became the national flag of Scotland and the martyr of Patras the patron saint. That too was how the bay became St Andrews Bay. Though people did not know very much about this far-off saint, everyone was agreed that his bones were potent.

But the stones and mortar of this ancient city are almost as old as its legends. On the Kirk Hill, overlooking the harbour, you can still see the foundations of a chapel that was built by Culdee churchmen before the Normans came to Britain. A King of Scotland, Constantine III, is said to have abdicated his throne in 942 A.D., because he

yearned to spend the rest of his life free from cares of state, in this lovely spot. He became a member of the religious community at this Church of St Mary on the Rock and for the last five years of his life he was the Abbot.

From the ruins of the ancient church the Long Pier can be seen far below, stretching out into the bay. And beyond the pier, on a rock that is now submerged, was a still earlier chapel that went back almost to the beginnings of Christianity in Scotland. Coastal erosion and quarrying drove the monks from that site and, wise from their experience, they chose the Kirk Hill instead. Not all the foundations on the hilltop, however, are part of the Culdee Church. Only the nave at the western end is as old as Constantine. The much larger chapel was added later, for this was a chapel which remained in use all through the Middle Ages. It was the Chapel Royal for a time.

There are other reminders too, in St Andrews, of the Dark Ages and the craftsmen who flourished just before the Danish sea-rovers came plundering along the coast. Some finely carved stones in the cathedral museum belong to that period — and one especially can stand comparison with the best in Dark Age Europe. It was no uncouth barbarian who carved this stone. The dress of the huntsmen, the horse's elaborate saddlecloth and the ornate dagger are all proof of that.

It was certainly the work of a Christian—one who had enjoyed studying the pictures in some Northumbrian manuscript of the Gospels. That would have given him inspiration for the figure of David wrestling with the lion. The still more unexpected apes could have come from the same source. And there are the decorative panels on each side of the hunting scene. One of these, showing animals with long sinuous bodies gracefully entwined, is typical of those Northumbrian manuscripts. But the sculptor did not choose just one source for his inspiration. He aptly reminds us that there were artists as well as wicked sea-rovers among the Norsemen, for some of the features of those panels are unmistakably Norse. Yet, in spite of that, the central theme of this impressive work of art is not International Friendship. It is Man the Intruder in a world of nature. And how those Picts loved to intrude! Even King David had to step aside, to let the huntsmen go storming into the middle of the picture, with sword and spear ready for the slaughter. The rich man on horseback, with his falcon on his wrist, and his hound running on ahead, is obviously hunting for pleasure. But the deer is not his only quarry. There are two foxes as well and the animal at the foot, on the left, is undoubtedly a wolf. There were plenty of wolves in Scotland in those days.

The stones were found about seven feet below ground level, when a grave was being dug in 1833. But we can be sure they were never intended to be hidden from view. At some time — perhaps when the Norse sea-rovers were raiding the coast—the grass grew over the grave. And the mouldering dust of nine hundred years accumulated after that, on this treasure of the Dark Ages.

If this Pictish sarcophagus is unique as a work of art, no less unique is St Rule's Tower, beside which it was found. This is a tower which still soars intact above the shattered ruins of the much later cathedral. Built in the romanesque style, with small round-topped windows and massive walls of fine-dressed masonry, it is the only one of its kind in Scotland. And it was not erected without powerful opposition. Five miles to the west, up at Drumcarro Craig, one giant was most annoyed. He borrowed his mother's apron and, using it as a sling, tried to knock the tower down with an avalanche of stones as they built it. Luckily for the masons he was foiled at the start, for his very first stone was too heavy. It fell far short, landing on the bank in Lumbo Den, where you can still see it. And, since the apron was burst in that mighty attempt, he could hurl no more stones at the tower.

[123]

Art is timeless in its inspiration.

[124]

The St Andrews sarcophagus.

Some geologists would try to persuade you that the great conglomerate boulder, 8 by 6 by 3 feet, was in the den for thousands of years before that particular giant lived up at Drumcarro Craig—that it was brought there by a glacier in the Ice Age. But who would believe the geologists, when you have a genuine living tradition like that!

Anyway, the masons who built the tower were masters of their craft. Once a great fire broke out halfway up, and enveloped it in flames and smoke. Inside you can still see where the flames bit several inches deep into the stonework. And outside, on the south wall, two stones are actually split by the heat. But the tower stood firm. Today it is still the striking landmark it has been for well over eight hundred years.

St Rule's Tower was already finished before the cathedral was begun in 1160 A.D. But after that, for the next century and a half, the stone-masons were seldom away from the site. By the end of the 13th century they had almost finished their cathedral. It was well over a hundred yards long and by far the largest ecclesiastical building ever to be erected in Scotland. But before it was even consecrated its long series of misfortunes began. In 1304 the army of King Edward I was besieging Stirling Castle and he needed lead for his war engines. He got twenty-two wagonloads from St Andrews, where his

[125]

soldiers stripped it from the roof of the unfinished cathedral and the priory houses. But Edward I had no quarrel with God. Next year he paid the prior £78 16s 2d in recompense and two months later he sent twenty oaks from the Forest of Clackmannan to repair any damage that might have been done to the priory houses. Those priory houses would have been built of wood. It was still the normal material for domestic purposes.

Before the cathedral was finished and consecrated, Bannockburn had been fought and won. King Robert the Bruce and almost all his nobility attended the consecration ceremony and all went well for the next sixty years. Then came calamity. A disastrous fire swept through a large part of the building and the stone-masons returned to start again on much of what they had already finished. Fifty years later, there was murder in the cathedral precinct. On the dormitory staircase, one evening before vespers, Canon Thomas Plater plunged a dagger into the heart of the reverend prior Robert of Montrose. They buried the prior in state and the canon in a dunghill. And so one of the ghosts of the cathedral was born. Then in 1409 there was an ominous accident, when part of the south transept collapsed in a great gale and masonry went crashing through the roofs of the buildings below. At that time the cathedral was not even a hundred years old! But then the years rolled past, with no more serious trouble. According to one traveller, it was still "a very large and beautiful structure" in 1549, on the eve of the Reformation.

There is a castle too, on a cliff overlooking the sea. From about 1200 A.D. until the Reformation, it was the home of the Bishops and later the Archbishops of St Andrews, and not even the cathedral itself was as dogged by misfortunes as was the castle. In the short space of forty years, during the Wars of Independence, it was destroyed three times. The second time, in 1336, two English lords rebuilt it. But they might have saved themselves the trouble, for next year the Scots "dang it doun" again. Only the foundations were visible for the next fifty years. In 1547 the rebuilt castle was again badly damaged and most of what can be seen today was erected after that. Yet in spite of its disasters, not all the early part has vanished. The base of the fore-tower unmistakably belongs to the early castle, the work of those two English lords in 1336. They built a new main entrance, which lasted for the next two centuries, and its blocked up doorway can also be seen. Inside this old tower are parts which may be even older, going back to the very earliest days of the castle.

Though St Andrews Castle was always

St Rule's Tower.

Ruined St Andrews Castle, once the home of the Archbishops.

the home of churchmen, by an odd twist of irony it possesses one of the most gruesome dungeons in any Scottish castle. And Scottish castles were notably uncivilised in that! Hollowed out of the solid rock, the bottle-dungeon in this bishops' palace is black as night and shaped like a bottle, with a drop of no less than twenty-four feet to the floor. A Black Friar was secretly murdered there. And several notable prisoners spent their last nights in it, on their way to the scaffold or the funeral pyre, for crimes political or religious.

There were other religious buildings in the town. The humble Black Friars and the Grey Friars each had a monastery. There were also two hospitals. And if you were a traveller seeking board and lodgings, you had to be sure that you did not go to the wrong one, the one on the outskirts of the town. It was a nursing home for priests who were dying of leprosy, the most dreaded of all diseases in the Middle Ages. Not even kings were immune from it. Robert the Bruce was one of its notable victims. By the end of the fifteenth century, advances in medical knowledge had almost stamped it out. Cases had become so rare that this hospital of St Nicholas was put to another use as a home for "crypallis, lamyt, blynd and pouir".

The hospital for the travellers was St Leonard's, close to the priory pends, and it was already established by the mid-twelfth century, long before there was any cathedral. Many a sick pilgrim was carried through its friendly door in the early days, when the bones of St Andrew were at their most potent and working wondrous miracles. People travelled long distances to his shrine, from England as well as Scotland, in the Golden Age of the 13th century when the two nations were still at peace. But somehow the holy relics began to lose their virtue and the number of pilgrims dwindled. By 1512 St Leonard's had ceased to be a hospital and it, like the hospital of St Nicholas, was put to another use.

There was a parish church too, for the cathedral, in spite of its size, was never the place where the townspeople worshipped. For three centuries up to the year 1410 the church was east of the cathedral site. But then the townspeople were gifted six rigs of land, with a frontage of 180 feet, in the heart of the town. And, ever since, the Church of the Holy Trinity has been on that new site in what was then known as the Southgait.

Even if the religious buildings had been all that St Andrews possessed of distinction, it would still have been an imposing city. But it had much more. By about 1400, Scotland and England were so often at war, with pirate ships lurking along the coast, that scholars

St Salvator's, the Auld College of the University, built by Bishop Kennedy in 1450.

Here, on North Street, we see two very different types of stairways.

became reluctant to risk the dangers of travelling to Universities overseas. A small Scottish university was founded at St Andrews in 1411 and it received the Pope's blessing soon after. Of all the universities in Britain only Oxford and Cambridge are older.

By 1450 it was still new but growing fast. That year Bishop James Kennedy—one of the most distinguished statesmen of his day—built St Salvator's College and a handsome chapel beside it with beautiful windows and a stone-vaulted roof. The frontage on North Street, except for the buttresses, is still very much as he knew it five hundred years ago. And there are other reminders, inside, of this famous Bishop. In the belfry is the original college bell, which he provided in 1461. Twice in its long history it has been cracked and recast, in 1609 and 1686. At first its name was Katharine but by 1686 even the Town Council were referring to it more familiarly in their minutes as "the Colledge Bell called Catharine Kennedy", and

now the "Catharine" has been contracted to Kate.

In the chapel vestry is another reminder of its founder — one of the treasures of St Andrews, the mace which Bishop Kennedy gifted to his college. It it still carried in all the University's ceremonial processions. And another treasure in the chapel too is the magnificent tomb which was made for him at Tournai in France about 1460.

His bones lie buried in the vault beneath, in a silver casket. And thereby hangs a tale. In 1930, when the chapel was being extensively restored, the gloomy vault was opened and the Principal and the architect went down with lamps to see the Bishop's coffin. As they stood beside it in the semi-darkness, there was a sudden ear-splitting report and the sides of the casket collapsed. And there in front of their eyes lay the skeleton of the Bishop. The bones were then made imperishable by modern science and they were returned to the vault in a new casket of silver.

Travellers entered St Andrews by guarded ways. The West Port.

In the early 16th century the University was still growing. That year the old Hospital of St Leonard, where the pilgrims had stayed, was refounded as St Leonard's College. And, a quarter of a century later, Archbishop Beaton started the building of a third college, St Mary's. His nephew, the Cardinal, continued the work. Loveliest of the three, St Mary's still retains its 16th century Founder's Tower and other early buildings, facing the University Library in the spacious quadrangle.

Mary Queen of Scots is said to have planted the thorn tree which still stands somewhat miraculously in front of the tower door. Its trunk is patched with plastic wood and steel poles support its branches. But still there is something of a phoenix about it, for in 1893 it was blown down in a gale and yet still it survives.

About the time when St Mary's College was being built, other improvements too were taking place at St Andrews. There had always been a wall round the 32 acres of cathedral precincts, but Prior John Hepburn early in the 16th century heightened this wall into something magnificent. From the Pends, the 14th century entry to his priory, it stretched down to the Sea-Yett which led to the harbour, then up along the edge of the cliffs and back round to the Pends, a distance of fully a mile. Probably, before he began, there were several

[132]

Queen Mary's Thorn Tree.

Louden's Close is a surviving example of an 18th century close in St Andrews.

corner turrets on the wall. There were thirteen by the time he was finished. And just in case posterity might forget who made this vast improvement, he had his coat-of-arms carved in at least nine different places along it. About the same time the Black Friars, with their old days of poverty forgotten, were building themselves a new monastery with a very handsome chapel alongside. There was wealth in St Andrews in those days. The Archbishop was said to be the richest man in Scotland.

With all this building going on for the Church and University colleges, the enthusiasm began to spread to the townspeople. Houses that had been good enough for their ancestors were no longer quite good enough for them. The old timber buildings with thatched roofs began to disappear and their place was taken by houses of stone with crow-stepped gables, and colourful red pantiles from the Low Countries on their steep-pitched roofs. The pantiles, so typical of the little houses of Fife, were shipped home as ballast in the local ships. And though the skippers had to pay for their ballast it was a profitable cargo. The demand from the house-builders was endless.

While the shipmasters, the small merchants and the master masons were building their handsome little houses, and starting a fashion which lasted for many a year, the merchant princes were busy too, erecting town houses like miniature castles, with turrets and moulding on the doors and windows, and roofs of dignified grey Angus slabs from the quarries of Turin. More often than not, it was the back of the house that faced the street, while the front looked down the long narrow rig of a garden. Often there was a doocot near the foot of the rig, to help the winter food supply, and even the doocot had to be picturesque, for beauty mattered in those days.

That was the time when the old St Andrews reached its zenith and by good fortune a picture map reconstruction gives us a good idea of what the town was like in those days around 1540. The Archbishop's Palace was much larger and more imposing then. It was badly damaged for the fourth time only some seven years later. The towering walls of the cathedral precinct, newly heightened by Prior Hepburn and bristling with towers, are clearly visible too. There are a few surprises, of course, like the spire on St Rule's Tower and the Eastern minarets on the Cathedral itself. We can be very sure the cathedral never had such minarets, though there is a certain similarity in the damaged west gable. But on the whole the map is accurate.

From the Cathedral the two main thoroughfares — the Southgait and the Northgait — swung westwards just as

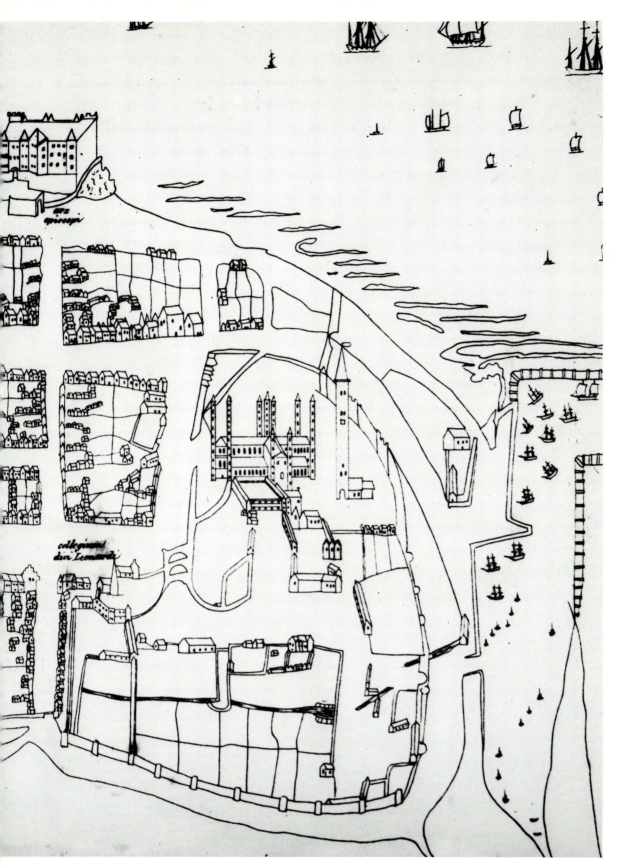

A picture-map representation of how St Andrews looked about 1530.

they do today, with the Marketgait between. And almost every house had its rig of land, with the largest mansions and the longest rigs at the Cathedral end of the Southgait and the Northgait. The little houses were chiefly crowded round the broad market place, the hub of the town's commercial life.

In the middle of the market place was the Town House, with the Market Cross beside it. And other things tended to be grouped around that focal point. The great parish church of the Holy Trinity was close by, in the background, and so too was the monastery of the Franciscan Grey Friars. All that now remains of their extensive buildings is the well from which they drew their water. The Black Friars monastery too, with its handsome new-built chapel, was only a short distance away.

The three University colleges are shown and named — St Salvator's, the oldest of the three, in the Northgait; St Leonard's, still very new, beside the Cathedral; and St Mary's, not yet finished, in the Southgait.

At the far end of the town can be seen not just one Port but three, for the Northgait and the Marketgait had theirs as well. Including those in the Cathedral's precinct wall there were no less than eight altogether. Though the citizens of St Andrews could never claim that they lived in a walled town, at least

they could claim with some assurance that no countryman would slip through the barriers on market day without first paying his Petty Customs. Those Petty Customs were abolished long ago and most of the gateways then vanished too. But the ground plan of the heart of St Andrews has changed remarkably little in the last four hundred years.

Life in those days was full of intoxicating promise, like the Golden Age of the thirteenth century. It was an age of good taste and refinement and a new-found wealth. But then some folk got drunk with power and the smell of blood began to dispel the promise.

The trouble began on Leap Year's Day, 1528, when the heretic Patrick Hamilton was tied to a stake and burned in the Northgait, just outside the College where he had taught his heresy. Burning in those days was a not altogether uncommon form of capital punishment. Only nine years later the beautiful Lady Glamis met the same fate on the Castle Hill in Edinburgh, on what everyone knew was a trumped up charge. But the mutterings about her wrongful death soon died down like the flames that consumed her. With Patrick Hamilton it was different. When his burning began about midday there were too few faggots and too little straw. The story goes that for six hours you could smell the acrid smoke as the fire was stoked and restoked in that botched burning. And even when the smell had vanished from the air, the crowds of onlookers could not so easily get rid of the memory. "The reek of Patrick Hamilton," it was said, "infected all it blew on."

Long afterwards his initials were designed in cobble-stones just outside the entrance to St Salvator's College close to where he died a heretic and lived on as one of the martyrs.

Henry Forrest was burned in 1533 and next to die was George Wishart, the most gentle of all those Scottish martyrs. He met his fate in front of the castle in 1546 and among the great crowd who watched was Cardinal Beaton himself, at one of his windows. Wishart's initials too can be seen, picked out in cobble-stones, on the roadway.

Last to die was the octogenarian Walter Myln, in 1558, scarcely a year before the Reformation reached its full momentum. Like Henry Forrest, he is said to have been burned on the Martyrs' Knowe, on the edge of the cliff just above St Rule's Cave. Soon after his death a great cairn was built to his memory. But it did not seem right to build a cairn to honour a heretic, so the authorities pulled it down. It was rebuilt and demolished again.

If you want to see what marks the spot of his martyrdom and that of Henry Forrest, you must go elsewhere — just north of the Cathedral to the entrance of Dean's Court, to a cross with a surrounding halo on the pavement. Here also they are said to have died.

In the Market Place is a similar cross, without a halo, to mark the site of the market cross. Beside it another heretic martyr died, about a hundred years earlier, the Bohemian Paul Craw.

And in The Scores, between the historic Old Course and the Step Rock Pool, is a ponderous Martyrs' Monument that was designed by a Government architect in 1842, as a tribute to all except Craw. No Martyrs died there, though witches were burned on a hillock close beside it. And their deaths were probably just as painful, and sometimes even less deserved.

Others too met a violent death in those bitter years of change and one of these was Cardinal Beaton, who regarded heresy as a deadly sin. Like the witches beside the Martyrs' Monument, no cobble stones have been laid for him. When he was killed in his castle in 1546, his Protestant murderers brought him "dead to the wall-head in a pair of sheets, and hung him over the wall by the tane arm and the tane foot, and bade the people see their god".

John Knox was not one of the murderers but later he joined them in the castle. And so he was able to record that they salted the Cardinal's lifeless

George Wishart died in front of Cardinal Beaton's palace.

body "to keep him from stinking", and threw it into the bottle dungeon. There it lay for seven months before it was buried at the new-built Black Friars' Convent in the Southgait. Eleven months later, six galleys and two great battleships arrived from France to get rid of the castle's unwelcome occupants and Knox spent the next two years as a galley slave.

By that time all hope of an imminent Golden Age for St Andrews was dead and gone. The Age of the Unco Guid was coming instead. And here it began somewhat earlier than elsewhere. In 1559 John Knox arrived back in Scotland and chose North Fife as the starting point for a whirlwind campaign to destroy the old Catholic Church. On 9th June he preached in Crail, on 10th

Where Paul Craw was put to death in the Market Place.

June in Anstruther, and from Sunday 11th to Wednesday 14th in St Andrews. In each place his theme was the same—that the time had come to eject the buyers and sellers from the temple. By the Sunday night the sound of breaking stones and tumbling walls was echoing through the cathedral city.

William Tennant, the Anstruther poet, went a little too far when he said that the mob —

> Gaed to Sanct Androis toun,
> And wi' John Calvin in their heads
> And hammers in their hands and spades,
> Enraged at idols, mass and beads,
> Dang the Cathedral down.

There were not enough demolition workers for that. But the altars, the statues and all the rich vestments and

[141]

Not much was left of Blackfriars Chapel after John Knox burned the monasteries.

religious treasures accumulated during the centuries were destroyed The wooden statues were set ablaze on the site of Walter Myln's martyrdom. Even the stone figures in their niches round the precinct walls were smashed into fragments. Only one Madonna has survived to modern times and it is mutilated.

Other buildings suffered worse than the cathedral. The Black Friars monastery with its chapel, where Cardinal Beaton had his belated burial, was visited on the Wednesday and "before the sunn was doune, there wes never inch standing bot bare walls". The Grey Friars monastery, less substantially built, was even more completely gutted. And the

chapel on the Kirk-Hill met a similar fate. All along the East Neuk and up the Tay Estuary the Reformers were laying their trail of havoc.

Lovely old Lindores Abbey was wrecked at that time. "We reformed them" was Knox's comment on that visit; "their altars overthrew; their idols, vestments of idolatry and mass books we burned in their presence, and commanded them to cast away their monkish habits." And though more than a year had still to pass before Scotland ceased to be a Roman Catholic country, soon there were many Catholic churchmen only too willing to obey his command. In February 1560 Dean John Wilson, vicar of Kinghorn, came to St Andrews of his own accord and vowed he would never let "that lecherous swyne the Byschop of Rome" have any authority within Christ's Church. Some twenty-six local churchmen also recanted at that time and a few days later, in the parish church, so did the Venerable John Gresone, in more moderate language, after fully thirty years as head of the Black Friars in Scotland.

It was not only churchmen who were changing their habits. In July the local Hammermen held a special meeting, for the rules of their craft had fallen out of date. It had always been one of the rules that when a member died, each of the others donated a plack and this was divided among the poor chaplains "for to pray for the saul of the said brother". And usually, when anyone broke a rule of the craft, he paid the penalty by providing some wax for the candles at the altar of St Eloy, where the Hammermen worshipped in the parish church. Now there were no altars, no burning candles, no curates praying for the souls of the dead. So these were dropped from the rules. And that happened a month before Parliament decided that Scotland was to be a Protestant country.

One might have expected a flood of new students at the University, now that so many parishes throughout the country were needing Protestant ministers. But there was no sign of that, at the start.

The numbers dwindled instead, to about half of what they had formerly been. The entire intake of freshmen in the whole University, during 1651 and the following year, was only 47 altogether.

But if it was lacking in numbers, there was at least no lack of a personal touch. The fatherliness of the teaching staff might seem almost embarrassing to a modern student. Among the bejants at St Mary's College, during the first hectic years of the change-over, was a certain Andrew Melville who quickly caught the attention of the University Rector. It was scarcely surprising. While the rest of the class read their Aristotle in English, he used the original Greek. And that was a language which even "his maisters understud nocht". On cold winter nights the Rector took Melville up to his study and sat by the fire with him. And rubbing the lad's hands and cheeks to warm them, he would tell him with a blessing: "My sillie fatherles and motherles chyld, it's ill to wit what God may mak of thie yit!"

We, of course, know what God made of him. It was this same Andrew who reminded James I in Falkland Palace that, though he was a King, he was still just "God's sillie vassal."

The privacy of the Rector's study was not the only place where University life was then slightly different from now. About ten years later another of the

Melvilles, nephew James, the future minister of Kilrenny, became a student at St Leonard's College. He arrived with a fair knowledge of golf, that he had learned at a private school run by a minister near Montrose. Not even St Andrews can claim, like this little school at Logie, to have brought golf into the educational curriculum so early.

But though James was rather good at golf, his grammar was depressingly bad. And trying to follow the Regent's lectures was almost as big a headache. So in the classroom he "did nathing bot bursted and grat at his lessons". Just when he had reached the point of wanting to rush back home, he found the Regent was just as fatherly as the Rector had been to his uncle ten years before. He took the boy up to his room each night and they sat side by side going over and over the day's work, until Melville "was acquented with the mater".

Students were younger in those days. The two Melvilles matriculated when they were under fourteen. But memories of their student days remained with them all their lives. James could remember the aged John Knox, staying at the Priory and coming across the road to speak to the boys in the courtyard of St Leonard's College. He remembered too the last time the old man came to preach in the town. In spite of his frailty he walked down the Southgait from the Priory to the parish church, every day, leaning heavily on his stick and with his servant supporting him on the other side. Two men were needed to help him up into the pulpit.

He would stand there for a minute, tottering slightly, as his strength came slowly back. His pulpit is no longer there but the church with its tower and its pillars inside is again very much as he saw it. His voice was low when he began, "bot or he haid done with his sermont he was sa active and vigorus that he was lyk to ding that pulpit in blads, and fly out of it!" A few months later he was dead.

For all his fire and vehemence, there were many in St Andrews by that time who disagreed profoundly with his teaching. There were even some, like the vicar of Kinghorn, who returned to the old religion in spite of all they had said before about "that lecherouss swyne the Byschop of Rome". And those in St Andrews who lacked the fire of Knox had some cause to feel disillusioned. With the loss of the Archbishop, the priests and the friars, of all their activities and the many buildings they maintained, St Andrews was suddenly deprived of by far its biggest industry. Trade had never been so slack. And even apart from local work, the town's sea trade was dwindling too, as the centre of commerce moved across the Forth or west to Glasgow. A new

The remains of the great nave of St Andrews Cathedral.

shabbiness was creeping into the dying town. While the masons and the wrights searched in vain for work, the two monasteries and the Kirk-Hill chapel still lay in ruins, with no hope of being repaired. The Cathedral too was in a dangerous state, for by that time it had been robbed of the lead on its roof, and the long north wall and the central tower could come crashing down at any time. No one had the money—even if they had the desire—to keep it from falling. St Mary's College, though so recently built, was "ruinous" by 1579, while by 1588 a quarter of the cloister of St Salvator's and the great hall above its school were also badly needing repair. Witches were being burned in St Andrews at that time. One of them, says the Kirk Session Register, "was accused of mony horrible thingis which she denyed, albeit they were sufficientlie proven". But the witches of St Andrews had no cause to complain. In other countries they were burning up, not in ones and twos but in tens and hundreds.

By 1580 the two Melvilles were back in the scenes of their student days and installed in St Mary's College, with Andrew the Principal of the University and the youthful James teaching Hebrew grammar. Completing the staff was John Robertson, who had been long at the college. He had made some study of Theology and was "a guid weill-conditionet man, but of small literature and giftes". St Mary's was the smallest of the three colleges. Only forty-nine students had matriculated there in the previous four years. But St Salvator's, in its ruinous state, had almost as few. St Leonard's, with 128 freshmen in the same four years, was bigger than the other two combined. And if this suggests that the University had a very small roll indeed, a century later it was even smaller.

The two Melvilles arrived just after St Mary's had been turned into a purely Theological College and extensive repairs were going on. They had scarcely moved in when a great load of timber, stored by the workmen in one of the cellars, went on fire—"to the joy of the wicked".

For a time it seemed that the whole building must be destroyed in the flames.

It was not by accident that James Melville, in describing that fire, referred to "the joy of the wicked". Long before the end of the century, St Mary's and the other colleges were at loggerheads with each other and even more with the townspeople and their civic fathers. Conditions were growing steadily more grim. The town's Common Good was almost exhausted. The pier and the harbour were at "the verie point of utter overthrow". And almost everyone was in the grip of poverty. There was little you could do about a thing like that, except forget your troubles in a game of golf or some archery at the Butts.

There had been a time, in 1457, when the Parliament of Scotland solemnly decided that "futeball and the golfe be utterly cryit doun" and that people must stick to archery alone. And that is the earliest record of golf in Scotland. But no one in St Andrews took the ban very seriously. By 1553 they had an inalienable right to play golf on the Links, just as they could shoot or play football or gather turf or pasture their livestock there. That was probably where James Melville's headmaster learned his golf. James himself continued to play when he arrived at St Andrews. His allowance from his father was not enough to let him join the drinkers at the tavern or take up real-tennis really seriously. But he had enough to keep himself equipped with "bow, arrose, glub and bals" for his archery and golf.

The displaced Roman Catholic prior and the canons of the priory had their golf too. No minister had been appointed to the parish church and in the late 1570s the Town Council was still letting the prior and his gentlemen-pensioners have the stipend and the kirk-rents. So they could afford to have some "goff, archerie, guid cheir, &c."

The townspeople were playing too — not only on ordinary days but also on Sundays and fast days, summer and winter alike. The Kirk Session was quite shocked to hear about Alex Miller's two sons. In December 1583 they defied their father and, with several "complices, playit in the golf feilds Sunday last wes, tyme of fast and precheing, aganis the ordinances of the kirk". Towards the end of the century there was a spate of church absenteeism, by people out on the Links, and by 1598 it was obvious that golf was the attraction. Two were brought before the Kirk Session in March that year, along with an adulterer and a pimp. After explaining that their "prophaning of the Saboth day in playing at the gouf eftir nune" was a first offence, they got off with an admonition.

Archers of the Queen's Bodyguard, the Royal Company of Archers.

But by the following year the trouble had spread to the Kirk Session itself. Then a list of fines was drawn up for those who "beis fund playand or passis to play at the goufe" when they should have been attending the Session meetings. It was 10s for the first offence, 20s for the second, public repentance for any addict bemused enough to do it a third time, and deprivation of all offices if he carried on any longer.

Archery was more of a gentleman's game, as it still is if you belong to the Royal Company of Archers. The townspeople were not too enthusiastic, in 1592, when some Theology students at St Mary's College built a pair of archery butts in the College garden, alongside the public wynd. One of the masters, more expert in religion than shooting, sent an arrow soaring over the butt and the thatched roofs of several houses beyond, to strike a maltster on the head as he was walking along the wynd. And that caused a riot. Someone rang the town's bell to summon the populace and soon a great crowd had smashed the

College gate and was battering at the door of the Principal's chambers. It was only after an ugly scene "and mikle adoe" that they went away, having been promised no more such annoyance.

Some of the townsfolk, in fact, were a sore trial to any decent God-fearing Presbyterian. They had customs that were positively pagan. You could actually see them, at a funeral, carrying the body round and round the church— three times altogether in the direction of the sun—to prevent the devil getting hold of the deceased. They were doing that kind of thing before Christianity came to Scotland and they were still doing it in 1641, when the Presbytery of St Andrews decided it must continue no longer.

The Cathedral's central tower and the north wall had both collapsed by that time. And when Cromwell invaded Scotland and killed or captured 13,000 Scots at the battle of Dunbar, in 1649, St Andrews Town Council was allowed to use the stones of the cathedral buildings and its walls and dykes, to fortify the

St Andrews Castle in the 1680's, soon after the slates and timbers were sold.

town. Every man's house was his castle. From then on, the cathedral became a quarry, for rich and poor alike, any time they had building in mind. It continued so for centuries. In houses all over the old town can be seen finely dressed stones, selected from the ruins of the cathedral. And that perhaps was not altogether a bad idea. Many of those houses lend their own special charm and dignity to the town today. St Andrews would be the poorer without them.

But still the decline continued. In 1655 the Long Pier collapsed in a storm and the Council had to sell the slates and timber of the castle to meet the cost of repairs. So, for the fifth and last time in its long history, the castle too became a ruin like so much else in the decaying town.

Even religion had sunk into a sorry state by that time. It was not the good life that took a man to heaven. You had to face the fact that if you believed in bishops—or vice versa—you might very well be damning your hopes of ever reaching the Promised Land. And bishops were a fact. For almost three-fifths of the seventeenth century the parish church of the Holy Trinity was an Episcopalian Church, like all the other parish churches throughout the country. The Primate of all Scotland was again the Archbishop of St Andrews. And few local people were greatly

A pyramid marks the dark place where Archbishop Sharp was murdered.

concerned about the small number of angry Protestants who were holding conventicles in secret places and ready to die for their faith. But soon the Covenanters of Fife could no longer be ignored. The Archbishop then was James Sharp, who had played a big part in turning Scotland back to Episcopalianism, almost twenty years before. Since then he had dabbled too much in politics to be widely popular. On 3rd May 1679 he was travelling back to St Andrews with his servants and one of his daughters after a visit to Edinburgh. The final stage of the journey was across Magus Muir.

He must have made the journey scores of times before. But this time nine local Covenanters decided that God had made them his executioners for sins against the true religion. They were not very good executioners. It took them three-quarters of an hour to drive the life finally out of his body, while his daughter vainly tried to save him. Later, one of the godly band of assassins described his closing minutes: "John Balfour struck him on the face, and Andrew Henderson stroke him on the hand and cut it, and John Balfour rode him down. Whereupon he, lying upon his face as if he had been dead, and James Russell hearing his daughter say to Wallace that there was life in him yet, in the time James was disarming the rest of the bishop's men, went presently to him and cast off his hat, for it would not cut . . . and hacked his head to pieces. William Danziel

The Covenanters' grave on Magus Muir.

lighted and went and thrust his sword into his belly." So the Primate of all Scotland died and his servants were told they could take their priest away.

A fortnight later, in the presence of a large congregation, the Archbishop was laid to rest in his church of the Holy Trinity at St Andrews, and two years later his son erected a magnificent memorial which can still be seen, over his tomb. Carved in Holland, of Greek and Italian marble, it even depicts his murder. And the Latin inscription tells how, in spite of all his gifts and qualities, he was murdered through the fury of fanaticism, "with many wounds from pistols, swords and daggers, while his eldest daughter and domestics, wounded and weeping, sought to protect him, and when he himself had fallen on his knees to implore mercy on their behalf."

Scotland remained an Episcopalian country for more than ten years after that and the spot where the archbishop died was not forgotten. Another

Ruins of the Cathedral in 1680. The cracks in St Rule's Tower already appear.

monument, a pyramid, was erected there. A wood now covers what was then the moor, but you can still see the cairn. Just beyond the third milestone on the B939 road to Cupar, at the Strathkinness crossroads a side road on the left leads to Peat Inn. A short way uphill on this road a signpost at a gate on the right points to the tree-shaded path which leads round the edge of the wood to "The Monument". You may, of course, return home having found the wrong monument. Five of the Covenanters who took part in the battle of Bothwell Bridge, seven weeks later, were captured and executed near this spot as rebels. They were buried in a field close to the path and in 1877 a stone wall was erected there with an iron railing on top and a gravestone inside. This is more easily seen than the Archbishop's monument, but his one is close at hand — a massive pyramid half-hidden from sight by its encircling yew trees.

It is said that on stormy nights, on the roads around St Andrews, you can still hear the Archbishop's phantom coach with its six horses thundering along to plunge into the waves of St Andrews Bay. That is a bad omen. It betokens a death!

* * *

The decay of St Andrews continued. By 1683 even St Rule's Tower was in danger of collapse. Massive crossbeams had been inserted — perhaps after the great fire—to hold it firm. But many of these had now been "sacrilegiouslie embezzled". St Salvator's too was in such disrepair that a hundred cartloads of stones were dug out of the castle walls for its repair. By 1697 the decay and destruction had reached such a stage that the professors tried to have the University moved to Perth. St Andrews, they pointed out, was now "nothing but a dirty village, the inhabitants of which were violently predisposed against the academicians". But at least there was golf. One of the professors admitted that St Andrews was "the Metropolis of Golfing".

Half-a-century later the University lost the largest of its colleges, when St Leonard's was combined with St Salvator's to form a new United College. And so the buildings at St Leonard's joined the lengthening list of neglected ruins in the town. Its tower was demolished soon after. But exciting things were happening in the world of golf. In 1754 some 22 noblemen and gentlemen, mostly land-owners in Fife, decided to move their golfing activities from Edinburgh to St Andrews, "the Alma Mater" of the game. And so the exclusive Society of St Andrews Golfers, the forerunner of the Royal and Ancient Golf Club, came into existence.

It was over a nine-hole course shaped like a shepherd's crook that they played —out to the crook and back along the same line. In their rules they referred to those nine holes out and nine holes in. And since those rules have since been adopted by clubs all over the world, what was an accident in St Andrews has become by design the rule in all other clubs.

Golf by that time was more than just a game in St Andrews. When the Town Council met each month for their deliberations, watching them from the wall was a portrait of the man who first went round the Old Course in 94, to set up a record which lasted from 1767 for the next 86 years. When the Council discussed the industrial situation, golf was again the theme. By 1772 it was providing the town with its only industry—the making of golf balls. And that brought heart-ache as well as pleasure. In stuffing the feathers in, you held the leather case against your chest, pushing with an iron rod, and almost everyone engaged in the industry died of consumption. But still St Andrews could thank its golf for the fact that in the next twenty years it did not finally turn into a Ghost Town. Two famous travellers have left their graphic impressions of the town in those days, when it came so close to becoming a city of the dead.

Thomas Pennant arrived in 1772 and his first impression was one of sheer

delight. Coming in from the south, he found the view magnificent, as he feasted his eyes on the many towers and spires, with the bay itself adding to the beauty of the scene. And then he came through the West Port and saw the "well-built street, straight and of a vast length and breadth". It was then he was so sadly disillusioned. South Street, he found, was grass-grown "and such a dreary solitude lay before us that it formed the perfect idea of having been laid waste by the pestilence". The towers and the spires, which looked so well from a distance, were ruinous on closer inspection. The harbour, once busy with its own merchant fleet, had now only one ship left that was local. . The population had dwindled to a mere couple of thousand. Even the University had reached the stage where its two colleges had little more than a hundred red-gowned students between them.

Next year Dr Samuel Johnson came on a tour with Boswell. And they got the same impression. To the doctor it seemed that even the ruins would soon be no longer visible. And that might be an advantage, for where was the pleasure in preserving such mournful memorials? He visited the University and found it pining in decay. And St Leonard's was past even that stage. Some excuse was always found to keep him out, when he tried to see the inside of its chapel. Later he heard that

Tommy Morris, golfer.

a vain attempt had been made to turn it into a greenhouse for the growing of shrubs and it gave him no pleasure to conjecture what use would next be made of it.

"It is surely not without just reproach," he added, "that a nation of which the commerce is hourly extending and the wealth increasing, . . . while its overlords or its nobles are raising palaces, suffers its universities to moulder into dust."

It was within the next few years that the phoenix was reborn. The reconstruction of the University Library's upper hall in the new classical style was one of the first signs that the old days of decay were passing. Even St Rule's Tower had its cracked walls repaired before the end of

the century at the expense of the Exchequer — though that perhaps was more with thoughts of its use as an invasion watch tower than as a legacy for posterity.

After the Napoleonic Wars the momentum quickened. New buildings were going up in the classical style and others no less handsome with a Jacobean air, in the old romantic tradition. Both took their place alongside the best of what was left of the old heritage. The town was growing in size and the University too, as the building boom continued. And the expansion still goes on. It is a far cry now from the days of the Melvilles, when in 1570 only 43 students matriculated. Four centuries later, in 1970, the matriculations in one year had grown to 2700. Today the town has been not inaptly described as a place where learning is almost the sole occupation.

But that, of course, is not quite true. Out in America, upwards of a century ago, a native of St Andrews recalled its other side —

Would you like to see a city given over
  Soul and body to a tyrannising game?
If you would there's little need to be a rover,
  For St Andrews is the abject city's name.
Rich and poor are smitten by the fever,
  Their business and religion is to play;
And a man is scarcely deemed a true believer
  Unless he goes at least a round a day.

R. F. Murray was not far wrong when he wrote those lines. By that time there were so many golfers that the course had to be enlarged to make room for them all. So the original greens were widened to take two holes instead of one, and a broader fairway was carved out of the heather and broom. On the outward half they played to a hole on the west side of the green and, coming back, to one on the east. The widening has continued since then, until now the fairways are three times as wide as they once were. And the double greens of the 1830s still remain as the unique feature of the Old Course today.

By 1834 the Society of St Andrews Golfers had become the Royal and Ancient Golf Club and then in 1860 golf became a way of life not only in St Andrews but elsewhere, when the first Open Championship was held to find the best golfer in the world. In the early days the competition was held not at St Andrews but at Prestwick. But Tom Morris of St Andrews went there. Four times in the first eight years he won the title and for 36 years, until he was well into his seventies, he was among the competitors each year. That was the golden age of golf in St Andrews—the age when golf to many people was the be-all and end-all of life.

There were giants among those golfers, though none of the others quite matched up to one of the sons of Tom Morris— young Tommy Morris. At the age of 17 he won his first professional competition in 1867 and next year he was the Open Champion. With an eleven stroke lead he won the title again in 1869 and in 1870 he increased his lead to twelve strokes, when he became the outright winner of the trophy, a red morocco belt richly ornamented with silver plate. It is now one of the golfing treasures in the Royal and Ancient Clubhouse. In 1871 there was no contest—a new trophy had not yet been provided—but that was remedied in 1872, and Tommy was again the winner for the fourth successive time. Between 1860, when the championship began, and 1872, he and his father had been the winners no less than eight times,

[157]

Golfers worldwide come to play at the Old Course, St Andrews.

a record never equalled since.

Three years later his life ended in tragedy. One September day, as the time drew near for the birth of his first child, he crossed the Forth estuary with his father to play in a challenge match at North Berwick. A telegram with news of his wife's illness brought the match to a sudden stop and as they were recrossing the firth and drawing in to the Long Pier at St Andrews, his father broke the news that his young wife and child were both dead. Three months later, on Christmas morning, Tommy also died at the age of 24. Sixty golfing societies contributed towards the memorial which marks his grave, close to St Rule's Tower in the Town Churchyard.

It was not all golf and education in St Andrews in those days, however. There was the ghost as well—the ghost in the haunted tower beside the cathedral. St Andrews fishermen, like all their kin, have been superstitious through the ages. They didn't like to meet a minister when going to sea or to hear anyone mentioning the word salmon or pig. And, whether going to the fishing or coming from it, they gave the haunted tower a wide berth. So, until recent times, when they landed their catch at the harbour, instead of going straight home by the cliff road, which passed close to the haunted tower, they chose a roundabout way, up through the Sea-Yett and round by the Pends, to avoid any encounter with the White Lady.

Most of the towers round the precinct wall are circular but this one near to the Turret Light, is oblong, with one little room at ground level and another above that is reached by a stone stair from the churchyard. An iron gate is on each doorway but it was not always so. For centuries the doors were close sealed and it was not until last century that someone broke into the lower chamber and found human bones inside. In 1868, the year when Tommy Morris first won the Open Championship, the upper room in this haunted tower was also opened, and almost a dozen coffins were found inside, piled on top of each other. You would almost have thought the bodies in them had been mummified. They were still well preserved and stiff enough to be set up on end if you had wanted. But the most remarkable thing of all was that one of them was the figure of a woman and she was still wearing white leather gloves just like the White Lady! The chamber was sealed up again and it was not until 1888 that the tower was again opened, the bodies disposed of and the iron grilles fitted on to the doorways.

The fishermen no longer go their roundabout way but death still hovers at times round the Haunted Tower, when herring gulls with an urge to die squeeze their way in through the iron bars.

The haunted tower in the Old Churchyard.

You get a feeling that someone is watching you at the Norman Church at Leuchars.

And isn't it odd that though St Andrews has been steeped in religion and religious feuds for so many long centuries, you have to go four miles out of the town to see the most delightful of all the churches in the district, the little Norman one at Leuchars.

It is one of the oldest in Scotland and, since the builders of the twelfth century had a mastery of their craft that has seldom since been approached, it is also one of the most beautiful. But even for a small Norman church it is exceptional. There is said to be only one other in the whole of Britain that might surpass it. Churches were built to last in those days. Almost five hundred years later it still stood firm when a lantern tower, that it was never intended to support, was built on top of the semi-circular apse in the 17th century.

The shafted arcading, on the outside of the apse and the chancel, is the special charm of this very lovely building and there is little doubt that it was designed by a churchman with a first-hand knowledge of architectural trends on the Continent. But the laird who supplied the money, regardless of cost, was a cosmopolitan too. The father of this Saier de Quenci was a Norman Crusader, while his mother was the daughter of a Celtic chief. This was his filial tribute to them.

[162]

10

In and Around Cupar

IN A county where most places take a pride in being old and historic, Cupar has always tended to cut out the sentiment and get on with the business, as befits a thriving county town. And business over the years has been good. A glance at the shops proves that. Few towns of its size have so many shops that cater for the connoisseur.

But Cupar, of course, despite all that, is a good deal older than most Fife burghs. In the heart of it, behind Bonnygate, is the Castlehill which played a long and notable part in Cupar's history. There the Thanes of Fife had their principal residence in ancient times and later it became the home of Sir David Lindsay of the Mount. Sir David was a dramatist with a devastating wit and one of his plays, "Ane Pleasant Satyre of the Three Estaits", earned him a more than ordinary fame. It had its premiere at an open-air performance on the Castlehill and soon was by far the most popular play of its day. Even now it retains its popularity, each time it is performed at the Edinburgh Festival.

The ancient Tolbooth was close to the foot of the Castlehill, until last century, when Cupar began to acquire its modern air. Then the civic fathers decided to widen St Catherine Street and the Tolbooth was one of several old buildings which stood in the way of progress. Not everyone relished the idea of pulling it down. There was a public outcry and an interdict was obtained. But that came too late. Before the objectors had time to serve the interdict, the improvers had the Tolbooth in flames. The Black Friars Monastery too was there, in ruins. What was left of it was also destroyed. Even the market cross, erected in 1812 to replace an older one, was uprooted and removed to Wemyss-hall Hill. But the cross was brought back in 1897 to mark Queen Victoria's Jubilee. It still stands today, bridging the centuries between the ancient narrow Bonnygate, with its old-world charm and the spaciously modern St Catherine Street on the other side.

There is contrast wherever you go in Cupar—in its wide streets and narrow pends, its ancient and modern buildings, and its attractive open spaces. This contrast is part of its character and nowhere is it more apparent than when you go up the narrow Kirk Wynd into the broad Kirkgate beyond, which is the very land of contrasts.

Here, as you might expect, are some houses with crow-stepped gables and decorative doorways. On one of the more modern houses, the ancient carved head of a bearded man looks moodily across at the parish church tower. The church is modern but the tower is fully 550 years old, with the remains of a rather lovely pre-Reformation church beside it.

Though the tower stands as sturdy as ever, it has seen some shattering changes. In early days its bell used to summon the devout Roman Catholics to mass. After that, for a century and a half, it was never quite sure whether the congregation down below was Reformed, Episcopalian or Presbyterian. They had such a habit of changing! And what made it even more confusing was all those finely carved monuments that marked the graves of their ancestors, round the kirkyard wall. It was odd how you could get so many different faiths, one after another, in a single family.

In 1680 there was a foretaste of another change. The authorities in Edinburgh were beginning to regard the town as among the worst in the whole country, for Covenanters, and so they sent it a souvenir for display after Archbishop Sharp was murdered.

It was really more a souvenir of David Hackston of Rathillet than of the Archbishop. Being a gentleman whose country estate was only four miles from Cupar, Mr Hackston was well respected in the town. But he became much more widely known, when he was put on trial and condemned to death, as leader of the gang who murdered the Archbishop. After he had been hanged, the authorities got the idea that maybe a relic of him could produce some miraculous change of heart in the hard core of the Covenanters. So

[164]

[165]

they cut him up, like one of the saints of old. Cupar got his right hand. And certainly something very odd did happen there after that.

The gruesome relic remained on show for several years, along with two Covenanters' heads that the town acquired in 1681. But eventually the Episcopalians lost their church and the Covenanters moved in. There was no need to keep the relics on view after that. David Hackston's hand and the couple of heads were buried in the churchyard near a little iron gate, well away from any mouldering Episcopalian dust, and a stone was erected to mark their grave. Above the inscription they put a carving of Mr Hackston's hand in the middle—and a head at each side with shoulder-length hair in the modern style. The inscription said nothing about the murder of the Archbishop. But it did explain, a little surprisingly perhaps, that Mr Hackston had been "most cruelly murdered in Edinr., 30th July, 1680," for "adhering to the word of God and Scotland's covenanted work of Reformation". And on the back of the stone they carved an eight-line elegy:

Our persecutors fill'd with rage,
Their brutish fury to aswage,
Took heads and hands of martyrs off
That they might be the peoples scoff

They Hackston's body cutt asunder
And set it up, a world's wonder,
In several places, to proclaim
These monsters gloryd in their shame.

Two old fonts have been placed at the corners of the kerb and an annual service is now held at the graveside.

Another interesting place near to Cupar is Ceres—only three miles south of the county town. It has been described as "the most attractive village in Scotland" and, even if you disagree about that, you will certainly admit it is one of the most attractive. Beauty is not its only charm. There is a uniqueness about it too—in its village green, its folk museum, its Ceres Derby, its Bishop's Bridge and its very delightful "Provost".

Tradition says that the village green and the ancient cobbled bridge have been there for more than 650 years—that the men of Ceres marched across the bridge on their way to the Battle of Bannockburn and on their return they celebrated their victory with games on the village green. The games are an annual event, on the last Saturday in June, with the Ceres Derby the highlight of the day's events. You may wonder, of course, why the old bridge is called the Bishop's Bridge and not the Bannockburn Bridge. But that is merely because the people of Fife have an obsession about Archbishop Sharp (and partly maybe because the bridge is really

A Bannockburn monument beside the village green recalls Ceres' proud history.

17th century). The Archbishop's coach passed over it on the way to Magus Muir. You may wonder too whether the games have really been held since 1314. The local folk have no doubt about that. There is a Bannockburn monument beside the green, where the ancient games are held.

Another rather special feature of Ceres is its folk museum. Housed in part of the Tolbooth and in some old cottages alongside, it recalls a way of life that has vanished from Scotland within living memory. In these modern times no play or novel is complete without its bedroom scene, and so this folk museum is right up-to-date. It has a bedroom scene so uncannily real that you almost apologise for the intrusion.

Part of the museum is in the Tolbooth dungeon and there you can see the thatching tools that John Brough used. He gifted them when he retired — a beater, a thatcher's knife and a needle almost three feet long. Beside them is a bundle of reeds nearly seven feet in height, from the Tay at Newburgh.

In the museum too is the figure of a piper, carved two centuries ago by John Howie, a local stone mason. Everyone in Ceres can tell you about him, for he also created the most lovable monument in the whole of Fife, his masterpiece "The Provost". This genial figure, rather like an outsize Toby jug, surveys the passing traffic at the Crossroads. It is said to be a caricature of the last ecclesiastical Provost of Ceres, appointed by James VI in 1578, and underneath is a panel in bas-relief of a cavalry skirmish. Mr Howie carved it on the gable-end of a 17th century building in Kirklands and for

In the Ceres Folk Museum.

The Provost of Ceres, Fife's best-loved monument.

years it was overgrown with ivy and forgotten. When it was rediscovered it was gifted to the village in 1939. "The Provost" and the piper are not the only works of this local stone mason. There is another figure by him on Saughtree Cottage.

Ten miles south-east of Cupar is Falkland, which has a unique place among old Scottish burghs. A royal palace, the favourite residence of many a Scottish king, is in the very heart of the town. As you walk along the High Street you can imagine yourself back in the days when most of the inhabitants were courtiers and retainers in the service of the king. And one of the surprises of Falkland is its apparent lack of class distinctions. All over Scotland, in the last two centuries, we have become accustomed to the fact that the rich live apart from the not so rich, and the not so rich from the poor. It happened not only in towns but in country districts too, where farm workers' cottages had to be round the corner and out of sight of the farmer's residence. Royalty at Falkland paid no heed to such niceties. In 1713 an unpretentious little house was built close beside the massive main entrance to the palace, and this house no doubt replaced an equally unpretentious one that stood on the site in earlier times. It was not only in house-building, however, that Stuart

James Stewart's engraving of the Palace and town, Falkland.

royalty was untroubled by class distinctions. Many a time you might have seen the king himself, playing on his beloved tennis court with one of the humbler members of his domestic staff.

This was royal tennis, known then as real tennis (*real* being the Spanish for royal). It was developed out of more ancient ball games as a complicated relaxation for kings and courtiers. Lawn tennis is its descendant. Played in a walled court, royal tennis calls for the speed and stamina of lawn tennis and squash, combined with strategical and optional hazards added, such as "touch no walls", "side walls" (must touch a side wall), "round service" (must touch a side and end wall), "half the court only", "bar the openings", "bar winning openings". For example, a shot clean through one of the holes in the court wall becomes an outright winner unless an opponent cries "bar winning openings" in time. The royal tennis court at Falkland was built in 1539 and is the second oldest in Britain after the first one made ten years earlier by Henry VIII in London. The game was originally played with the hand, not with racquets, and it was not until the next century that nets were introduced, replacing a fringed or tasseled rope. The court at Falkland continues in use today and interested parties may apply.

Falkland houses are familiarly adjacent to the Royal Palace.

The palace is by far the grandest building in Falkland. By any standard it is exceptional. And its variety of styles is part of its charm. Facing the street the south front is splendidly Gothic with its buttresses, its niches and statues of Christ and the saints. But the magnificent court-yard frontage in the classical style, with its pillars and medallions, strikes an entirely different mood with its air of gracious living. Scotland has few surviving buildings that were in the main stream of Renaissance architecture. But here is one, far and away the best of them all. And though it has strong French influence, there is a flavour about it too that is unmistakably Scottish. Most of the existing palace was built in the early 16th century by James IV and his son James V.

Falkland Palace was a well loved place where the Stuart kings and queens spent some of their happiest days. Yet the best known event that happened there was the tragic death of a king. James V was only thirty when he died of a broken heart on hearing of the birth of a daughter, the future Mary Queen of Scots. And it must have been galling, in those days of sex inequality, to have a daughter as heir to the throne, when he had already fathered three handsome sons by different mistresses. When the news was broken to him, "the King inquired whidder it was a man or a woman. The messinger said it was ane fair dochter. The King answered and said, 'Fareweil, it cam with ane lass and it will pass with ane lass'; and so he commendit himselff to Almightie God, and spak little from thensforth, but turned his back to his lordis and his face to the wall." And so he died.

More than three centuries have passed since the last of the kings left Falkland

There are not many real tennis courts like this in the world.

Richard Cameron's house.

but it is still a delightful town. Even the roofs of the houses are out of the ordinary. The palace is roofed with heavy grey slabs that came from an Angus quarry. A neighbouring house too has Angus slates, with heavy beams to support their weight, while the house next door has lightweight pantiles that were made in a brickworks. Just across the road is another old building, covered with stapled thatch for which the reeds were cut on the bank of the Tay at Newburgh. And, of course, there are houses roofed with blue slates. Four different styles, all close together! We shall see more thatched houses when we reach Auchtermuchty.

As interesting as the roofs of Falkland, and in some ways much more intriguing, are its Covenanters. The very word conjures up thoughts of secret conventicles on lonely hillsides, with guards maintaining a ceaseless watch in case the Govern-ment troops might surprise them. To be caught worshipping God at one of these could mean imprisonment or shipment to the colonies or even a sentence of death. No one would have dreamt of admitting to any stranger that he or she was a Covenanter.

So there is a special interest in the Covenanters' Bar which faces the Square in Falkland, only a stone's throw from the Royal Palace. It would be pleasant to think that in this royal burgh the faithful did not need to go out to the fields — that they could sit with their tankards in their favourite howff and make the rafters ring with their hymn-singing, while the garrison in the guard-house across the road turned a deaf ear to their tuneful refrains. But that is not very likely. The best they could hope for in Falkland was some secret rendezvous, where they could lurk in dark corners and work out their plans for a better Scotland. There was Richard Cameron, for example. He was born along the road in a handsome house where a plaque now says: "This is the house where Richard Cameron was born—Covenanter Martyr." He was not the kind of person who made casual friends easily. Most of the townsfolk in his day were Episco-palians and time after time he had warned the faithful that to be Episco-palian was a deadly sin — that the fellowship of all such must be utterly

Handsome is the word for Auchtermuchty's Tolbooth, built in 1728.

The thatched cottage tells us that the "theeker" plied his ancient craft here.

shunned. He was inclined to be a revolutionary too. He kept urging his people to rise up against Charles II and depose him. But Mr Cameron practised what he preached. He was killed in a skirmish with Government troops at Airds Moss. And that is how he became a martyr.

*   *   *

Less than four miles from Falkland is Auchtermuchty, the only town that stands astride the main road from Edinburgh to Dundee. As you pass through, you will have to turn up into the High Street if you want to see the heart of the town and the best of it. There you will find the Tolbooth and many another attractive building. At the far end is Braehead House, with the year 1712 on its lintel and a rounded gateway outside, much older than that. Four hundred years ago this gateway was erected as the courtyard entrance to a mansion in the town and it was later brought to its present position.

Next to Braehead House is the trimmest thatched cottage in Auchtermuchty. You might almost call it a memorial, for it was thatched by John Brough and he was the last reed thatcher in Scotland who plied his ancient craft. He came from Newburgh to settle in Auchtermuchty and during a long life as a master "theeker" he trained several young apprentices. But none stayed in the trade, to carry on after he retired. Now if you want a well thatched roof that will last you sixty years, you will have to go to Norfolk for a thatcher.

Oddly enough, though John Brough spent his life thatching roofs for others, he never did it for himself. He lived in a council house with a roof of blue slates and there he died in his eighties early in 1972. There will be fewer

A remarkable formation—the Bannet Stone, Maiden's Bore, and Maiden's Bower.

thatched houses in Fife, now that he is gone. And in this age of uniformity even pantiled roofs are becoming fewer.

*   *   *

Near to the centre of the Kingdom lie the tall Lomond Hills. They dominate the landscape of Fife from all quarters. It was from their height that King James I observed the "beggar's mantle fringed with gold" of salt-pan fires on the Firth of Forth and, if he had turned around, the Firth of Tay to the north. Falkland and its royal palace lie safely in their north shadow. And Auchtermuchty lies a bit away from them, north-east.

There are two romantic tales told of these hills . . . and two old rocks upon them to support the telling. The first tale is sad. At the grassy base of West Lomond and beyond any marked footpath, directly south of Gateside, is the Maiden Bower rock. One afternoon as she waited for her sweetheart, a young maiden watched in helpless horror as retainers of her disapproving father waylaid and murdered him. She vowed to remain at their trysting place, never to return to her father. She passed her whole life at the cave and became known as a saint who consoled the sorrowful and bereft. It is said that whoever visits her bower with a pure heart will have their wish granted within the twelve-month.

The second tale is wishful, too, but much less sad. Let the Reverend A. Small tell it to you as he first did in 1823: "There is a large perforation through the rock called the Maiden-bore. Maidens only were supposed capable of passing through it. The passage, originally very small, is now so enlarged by people trying to creep through that it will now admit the bulkiest." Very wishful, indeed!

[177]

The River Tay is the northern boundary of the historic Kingdom of Fife.

11
North
to
the
Tay

TURNING NORTHWARD at Gateside away from the hills that sheltered the maiden and Falkland Palace, we journey by the back ways to the north-east corner of the Kingdom. There Newburgh still has its reeds growing along the bank of the Tay, although it is better known for the orchards that clothe its upper slopes. It has long been noted for fruit trees. The Benedictine monks in the Abbey of Lindores on the outskirts of the town were famous fruit-growers and more than one Scottish King sampled the apples and pears of Lindores while in residence at Falkland Palace.

Adjacent to Newburgh are the ruins of the Abbey, founded by David, Earl of Huntingdon, in the twelfth century. The Abbey was dedicated to St Mary, and monks were brought from Kelso to establish it. Later Earl David founded a church in Dundee dedicated to St Mary. His brother, King William the Lion, had granted a Royal Charter to him, elevating Dundee into a Burgh.

Earl David gave the new church of St Mary in Dundee into the care of the Abbots of Lindores, who were charged with building and maintaining it and appointing its Vicars. In the 15th century an agreement was drawn up between the Town Council of Dundee and the then Abbot of Lindores, whereby the Town took over the responsibility for building and completing the Church of St Mary.

Like Brechin, in Angus, Abernethy has a thousand-year-old Round Tower.

So little now remains of the famous Lindores Abbey.

This agreement was signed by the two parties in the presence of and witnessed by the Archbishop of St Andrews.

Not much of the great 12th century abbey now remains—only the gateway and part of the tower and fragments of the great walls. But in its prime, with its red and white sandstone, it was famed almost as much for its beauty as it was for its adders. There is some doubt about what happened to the adders. According to some, the soil was replaced with consecrated earth brought specially from Ireland to keep them away. But Sir James Balfour has a more dramatic version in the annals he wrote over three centuries ago. By 1330, according to him, the monks' sleeping quarters were teaming with such a plague of adders that the Virgin Mary herself took pity on the monks and drove the adders out. Yet they can't

have been entirely unbearable. Alexander III, Edward I of England and Sir William Wallace all enjoyed the abbey's hospitality when the adders were there.

No one, however, was able to get rid of John Knox and his "Congregation of the Godly" when they arrived in 1559 on the eve of the Reformation. There was little that twenty Black Monks could do against so many. "We reformed them," Knox tells us; "their altars overthrew; their idols, vestments of idolatry and mass books we burned in their presence, and commanded them to cast away their monkish habits."

The abbey never recovered from that visit. Its ruins became a quarry whenever any building stone was needed round about. But the fruit trees still grew on. Two and a half centuries later it was recorded that the remains of the orchard could still be seen and "some

Only fragments survived the demolishing of Carpow by the Romans as they withdrew.

All that the Romans left behind of the south gate of Carpow.

varieties of apples here exist which are nearly unknown to modern horticulturists."

Its pear trees, planted with slabs of stone beneath, were famous too. Almost two centuries after the monks had gone, John Sibbald, the father of Scottish botany, was amazed to see the "vastly big old pear trees still flourishing". Long after Sibbald's day they were still there. In 1876 Dr Laing saw one of them "eighteen feet in circumference, still bearing large crops".

The abbey, however, was not the only place in Newburgh famous for its fruit trees. The whole of Newburgh has long been noted as an orchard town with fruit gardens round its cottages and villas alike.

Only a hour's stroll from Newburgh is another ancient town just beyond the Fife boundaries in Perthshire — Scotland's ancient capital, Abernethy. It still retains a relic of the days of its greatness in a 1000-year-old Irish tower in the heart of the town.

The story of Newburgh, however, goes back far beyond its fruit trees and its abbey. It was only in 1178 A.D. that the monks arrived. A thousand years earlier, history was already being made on the western outskirts of the town at Carpow. The Romans called it Horrea, "The Granaries". The Roman army lived mainly on grain, and it has been estimated that a crop of about 70 acres was consumed by a Legion in one week.

At Carpow, near the narrowing of the waters of the River Tay, the Romans built in 208 A.D. a great fortress, a supply base and perhaps a floating bridge. It was to be the centre of their punitive campaigns against the tribes in Angus and Mearns. This military enterprise was so important that it brought Emperor Severus and his sons Caracalla and Geta with the imperial family to the Scottish hinterland from Rome to direct the Legion VI Victrix against the Maeatae and Caledonii. These were the

[183]

Traces of the hill fort are seen around the top of Norman's Law.

principal tribes north-east of the Antonine Wall which ran across the narrow waist between the Clyde and the Firth of Forth. The Romans were later in the century to use the collective name Picti for these tribes. Like nearly everything else connected with the Picts, it is not yet known what these people called themselves.

The expeditions to punish and subdue the northern tribes were conducted by Severus until he fell fatally ill. Caracalla took command and pressed the campaign to victory. He then returned the imperial household to Rome, continuing his bloody ways by murdering his brother Geta and 10,000 of Geta's followers to consolidate his own power as emperor. The fortress at Carpow was eventually demolished by the Romans when they withdrew to the south. There is evidence that they returned on a brief campaign to the north in 306 A.D., but Scotland was never Romanized as was England.

During the last decade there have been several seasons of archaeological excavation at Carpow. The site of the fort was carefully uncovered, measured, photo-

At Balmerino, the gentle mood of the Abbey lingers on.

graphed and recorded. The finds from these excavations are housed in Dundee Central Museum.

The narrow crossing of the Tay at Carpow could probably have been used by people before the Romans. Later it was used notably by Macduff as he fled from Macbeth. Even later, it was used by lesser folk until its ferry was overcome by modern ways.

But the evidence of human settlement around Newburgh extends back many centuries. For example, people built and lived in the hill-fort on top of Norman's Law during the last four centuries B.C. Today its remains are accessible by public footpaths from the motor roads north and south of the Law. Three circles of fortification can be traced clearly on the Law. The inner one crowns the summit with thick walls in an oval 170 by 100 feet.

Another fort was on the summit of Clatchard Craig, just behind Newburgh. It was clearly visible for well over two thousand years, until in modern times a quarry began to bite deep into it.

Sixteen hundred years later and five miles east of Norman's Law, a saintliness flowered for 300 years at Balmerino Abbey. This peaceful site was chosen in 1225 by Ermengarde, widow

An expert view by Dundee Museum of early fishing encampments on Tentsmuir.

of William the Lion. Her son, King Alexander II, gave her generous gifts to finance the building and on her death seven years later, Ermengarde was buried before the high altar. Little of the Abbey remains today. Warring times returned. In 1547 the Abbey was set on fire by an English army and in 1559 John Knox and his Reformers completed the destruction on their way back to St Andrews after reforming Lindores. Some of the pillars and part of the cloisters remain, however, and in the orchard is a great Spanish chestnut tree planted by the monks and now some 700 years old. Balmerino was described by King James V's physicians as having "the best airs of any place in the Kingdom".

East again from Balmerino another four miles is the north-south motorway speeding busy mankind between Edinburgh and Dundee. The same distance beyond the motorway we come to what makes all those other events seem only yesterday. Only 25 years ago, on a site near Morton Farm on the Tentsmuir Peninsula, evidence was found of a settlement visited seasonally by fishing and hunting folk about 8000 years ago.

This remarkable site is one of the early habitations in Scotland by man. It has been known only since 1957. It was first scientifically opened in 1963. About 6500 B.C. (that is, 8500 years ago) the sea levels around Britain began to

The very isolation of Tentsmuir shore gave haven to the Stone Age incomers.

rise and the climate warmed as the ice sheets melted from the land. Forests grew and migration of hunters and fishers began. It is possible they could still cross from Europe on land before Britain was isolated by the rising seas.

When their ancient abode in Tentsmuir was opened in 1963, more than 400 characteristic stone implements of those days were found. Among them were small, sharpened weapon tips, scrapers and cutters, made from pebble flint, quartz, agate, chalcedony and other semi-precious stones, all collected locally. Finds from the site are in the Dundee Museum and the National Museum of Antiquities in Edinburgh.

Information about these early folk is sketchy, but enough is known from the layering of refuse in middens to indicate seasonal camping for over 700 years. Their encampment was on a raised sandy promontory, a refuge surrounded by the sea during high tides. And where did they go after 700 years? Probably it was a change in life-style. They may have just stopped coming to Tentsmuir. Maybe they migrated permanently to another part of Fife to evolve into an early farming community. It is anyone's guess.

In the 8000 years' interval their sandy

At Leuchars, Norman artistry in stone is different from that at Dunfermline Abbey.

promontory has been absorbed into an expanded peninsula and is away inland. The peninsula, still a remote place, is partly farmland and partly covered with cultivated forest. And just north is the Morton Lochs Nature Reserve, where the wildfowl and waders are a sight worth seeing at migration time. To the east, along the coastal strip, is the much larger Tentsmuir Nature Reserve, which covers more than 1200 acres. Here the wildfowl roost in winter and it is a favourite haunt of seals. But expert naturalists go mainly to see what is happening to the plant life on the coastal sands, for all sorts of unexpected things happen there too.

The wonder of Tentsmuir completes our circuit of Fife, geographically from the south-west corner to the north-east, and historically from medieval Culross to those Mesolithic beginnings on the northern shores of the Kingdom. But if you are not yet content, you may travel south to cross the River Eden and linger once more in St Andrews or turn aside at Leuchars to visit again one of the most notable Norman churches in Britain. For in the Kingdom of Fife, history is always only a step away.

INDEX

[190]